WHILE GREEN GRASS GROWS

MEMOIRS OF A FOLKLORIST

BRÍD MAHON

MERCIER PRESS

Thanks to Professor Séamus Ó Catháin, Head of the Department of Irish Folklore, UCD, for permission to include photographic material from the folklore archives.

B. M.

First published in 1998 by
Mercier Press
PO Box 5 5 French Church St Cork
Tel: (021) 275040; Fax: (021) 274969
e.mail: books@mercier.ie
16 Hume Street Dublin 2
Tel: (01) 661 5299; Fax: (01) 661 8584
e.mail: books@marino.ie
Trade enquiries to CMD Distribution
55A Spruce Avenue Stillorgan Industrial
Park Blackrock County Dublin
Tel: (01) 294 2556 Fax: (01) 294 2564

© Bríd Mahon 1998

ISBN 1 85635 206 4

10 9 8 7 6 5 4 3 2 1

A CIP record for this title is available
from the British Library

Cover design by Penhouse Design
Printed in Ireland by ColourBooks,
Baldoyle Industrial Estate, Dublin 13

WHILE GREEN GRASS GROWS

This is the story of a dream, of a quest for the remnants of a once great civilisation, that will never again be known 'while green grass grows and rivers run'. The written literature of medieval Ireland has been described as 'the earliest voice from the dawn of Western civilisation'. Earlier still is the oral tradition and an oral literature preserved by poets and storytellers down to our own times. This book is an account of how a small group of people, working on a slender grant, managed over a period of a little more than thirty years to assemble the largest and most important body of folklore in western Europe. It is also a picture of life in Ireland during those years and of some of the men and women whose paths crossed in the search.

With love and gratitude to Brian and Marie-Thérèse
Farrell, who first suggested that I write
While Green Grass Grows

CONTENTS

INTRODUCTION

WHILE GREEN GRASS GROWS

Most people, if they think of him at all, conjure up a picture of Douglas Hyde (1860–1949) as an old man with a walrus moustache who by some quirk of fate became the first President of Ireland. Yet in his time he was a person of great significance to the Irish nation and a man of vision and charm. When in 1890 he published *Beside the Fire,* a book of folktales which he had collected mainly round his home in Frenchpark, County Roscommon, he dedicated it to friends of his youth: 'those truly cultured and unselfish men, the poet-scribes and hedge-school-masters of the last century and the beginning of this . . . the men who may well be called the last of the Milesians'.

An early illness had prevented young Hyde from being sent to school in Dublin. Instead he took morning lessons in Latin and Greek from his father in the rectory in Frenchpark, which left his afternoons free to fish the waters of Lough Gara and to shoot snipe in the bogs with boys who knew no English and whose culture, traditions and lifestyle were alien to his own. At night he was made welcome in their homes in the bog huts and cottages

8

where he heard his first folktales. But for that accident of fate, Douglas Hyde would probably have taken holy orders and lived the life of an Anglo-Irish gentleman. As it was, at the age of twenty he enrolled as a student in Trinity College Dublin, and thereafter everything he wrote and did was influenced by his burning passion for Irish folklore and the Irish language.

In the preface to *Beside the Fire* Douglas Hyde wrote:

Ten or fifteen years ago I used to hear a great many stories but I did not understand their value. Now when I go back for them I cannot find them. They have died out and will never again be heard on the hillsides, where they probably existed for a couple of thousand years; they will never be repeated there again, to use the Irish phrase, 'while green grass grows or water runs'.

While his fellow Anglo-Irish gentry complained that he had let the side down by mixing with the peasantry and speaking Irish, the ardent young folklorist and scholar made a great hit with Lady Augusta Gregory (1852–1932). She invited him to Coole Park and enlisted the help of a couple of Irish-speaking schoolteachers to help him in his work. He collaborated with her and W. B. Yeats (1865–1939) in writing plays, and the poet praised his collection of folktales as having 'the beautiful English of Connacht which is Gaelic in idiom and Tudor in vocabulary'.

Like almost every man of his time, he was bowled over by the youthful Maud Gonne, who was described by *The Times* as 'the most beautiful woman in Europe'. Yeats fell in love with her at their first meeting and she was to become the poet's inspiration and muse for most of his life. In the early summer of 1946 I visited her in Roebuck House, Dundrum, where she was living out her last years, in the company of my friend Áine Ní Chonaill, who was teaching her grandchildren Irish. Madame, as we called her, who was then about eighty, sat straightbacked in her chair, at her feet her beloved Irish wolfhounds and above her head the remarkable portrait she had painted of her daughter Iseult. I had brought her a book of fairytales I had written and Áine read aloud 'Deirdre and the Sons of Usna' which had always been Madame's favourite legend. She still bore the traces of great beauty but her once translucent skin was incredibly lined and I though sadly of Yeats's lines:

When you are old and grey and full of sleep,
And nodding by the fire, take down this book,
And slowly read, and dream of the soft look
Your eyes had once, and of their shadows deep

After their meeting Hyde would write in his diary:

To the Sigersons in the evening where I met the most dazzling woman I have ever seen. Maud Gonne drew round her every male in the room. We stayed talking until the early hours, my head spinning with her beauty.

He gave her lessons in Irish and tried to interest her in folklore but as she was to say later: 'Douglas Hyde never succeeded in making me an Irish speaker, any more than I in making him a revolutionary.'

When the National University of Ireland was set up in 1908, Douglas Hyde was appointed first Professor of Modern Irish, a chair he would hold for twenty-three years. One of Hyde's students, Séamus Ó Duilearga (1899–1980), a red-haired young man from Cushendall in County Antrim, was so fired with his professor's passion for folklore that he determined to begin his own odyssey. In the spring of 1923 he took the road that led him to Cillrialaig, Baile'n Sceilg, in the barony of Iveragh, County Kerry. Cillrialaig was nothing more than a cluster of whitewashed fishermen's cottages hanging between sea and sky. Even today it remains a remote, windswept place, set down in some of the wildest and most dramatic scenery in Ireland. Southwest lies Beara peninsula and the islands of Scariff and Deenish, and eastwards beyond Waterville Macgillicuddy's Reeks pierce the clouds. It was here that Séamus Ó Duilearga discovered the storyteller who was to be the inspiration for his life's work.

At the time of this meeting, Seán Ó Conaill was a gentle, dignified man of seventy years, who stood six feet tall and hadn't a wrinkle on his face nor a grey rib to his hair. The cottage in which he and his wife lived was modest: a kitchen, a bedroom and a loft containing a spare bed, fishing-gear, a spinning-wheel and the usual bits which might one day come in useful. Before the night's storytelling began, Séamus had his duties to perform. He swept the floor, brought in armfuls of turf, lit the oil lamp and chased out the hens which had hopped in over the half-door. On the kitchen hearth a turf fire blazed summer and winter. There were a couple of stools and a bag for salting fish on which Séamus seated himself, pulling to his side the well-scrubbed table on which he could write from Seán's dictation. Neighbours would drop in singly and in small groups, the magic opening words of the story, '*Fadó, fadó*' ('Long, long ago'), drawing them like a magnet. The sound of the sea which crept into the kitchen was the ever-present background to the folktale. When the story was finished Seán would take a burning ember from the fire, light his pipe, lean back in his chair and accept the congratulations of his listeners.

Over the years Séamus would visit that southwest corner of County Kerry every spare minute he could escape from his teaching job in UCD. 'Sometimes Seán would be waiting for me at his door,' he said. 'Sometimes I took him by surprise but his welcome was always warm: "God be to your life and your health. Come and sit by the fire."' In Seán's youth storytelling was popular in the district but there came a time when few bothered to listen. So, lest he forget the tales he loved, he would go out into the fields alone at night and repeat them to a tree or bush, using all the actor's tricks of voice and hands as if he were once again the centre of a fireside group.

The last meeting of the storyteller and his disciple came eight years, almost to the day, after the two had first met. To the sobbing of the wind tearing round the house, struggling to lift the ropes that secured the thatch, and the sound of the sea battering the rocks below, Seán Ó Conaill began his last folktale. It was very late by the time he had finished. Outside the wind had died down, the sea was quiet and the land all luminous under the moonlight,

1

THE OLDEST FOLKTALE IN THE WORLD

The first things I noticed were the wicker basket heaped with sods of black turf beside an open fire and the smell of blue peat smoke which I love. It was my first day as a raw recruit to the staff of the Irish Folklore Commission. One wall of the room was lined with manuscripts bound in dark leather. A small dark man was turning the handle of a machine. Shreds of wax from a long cylinder fell into a container. Seán O'Sullivan (1903–96), who was the archivist, explained that the wax cylinders he was paring were used by the collectors on clockwork dictation machines called Ediphones to record the tales and traditions of the Irish countryside. He said they were a great improvement on the old method of taking down information by hand. The only drawback was that the Ediphones had to be carried by the collectors on bicycles, which made riding over stony roads difficult and up mountains paths near impossible.

The Second World War was drawing to a close, petrol was scarce and few people owned cars. The Commission employed five full-time collectors, who worked in places as far apart as the Dingle peninsula in County Kerry and the Bluestacks in County Donegal. When the men had filled a dozen cylinders they transcribed the information into blue notebooks, using indelible ink. These were sent back to Dublin, carefully packed in boxes. The notebooks were bound and kept in the Commission's archives and the cylinders were pared and recycled.

Seán O'Sullivan showed me an international folktale known in Irish as '*Ao Mhic an Bhradáin agus Ó Mhic an Bhradáin*' ('Hugh and O, the Two Sons of the Salmon') which relates how a barren woman gives birth to two boys after eating a magic salmon. When the boys grow to manhood the elder sets out to seek his fortune, meeting a beautiful woman who turns him into stone. Later the second son goes in search of his brother, finds the enchantress, outwits her and saves his brother. A simple story, you might think, but what fascinated me was that it was the earliest known folktale, first discovered on Egyptian papyrus 3,250 years before. During my years with the Commission hundreds of variants of that far-flung story were gathered in remote hamlets on the western seaboard of Ireland, in parts of Munster, in northwest Ulster and from a group of travelling people on the borders of Wicklow and Wexford.

Another international folktale started life as a rumour. Herodotus, the Father of History, who was born about the year 484BC in the Greek city of Halicarnassus, was an inveterate traveller. While on a visit to Egypt he heard that the pharaoh's treasury had been robbed by means of a trick. The culprit was even named as Rhampsinitus, a well known thief. Herodotus was sceptical, but true or false the story spread across the world. Over 2,450 years later hundreds of versions of that same story were being recorded in Irish by our collectors. I often speculated as to how such tales first reached our shores. Were they carried across the sea by early settlers? Perhaps they were recited by a bard at a feast held in a princely palace with bronze doors and walls of carved wood, whispered to each other by Christian monks at work in the silent scriptorium of a medieval monastery, remembered by fishermen who kept themselves and their companions awake with stories during long nights at sea; told for the last time by one of the dying breed, the *seanchaí* or storyteller. Small wonder I became hooked on folklore – the search, the clues, the earliest known sighting of a tale or tradition – all proving how tenacious is man's memory. It was no surprise to learn that Séamus Ó Duilearga's favourite bedtime reading was detective stories.

Séamus Ó Duilearga, or James Hamilton Delargy as he was known to his family and friends, boasted that he had an unerring gift for picking the right man or woman for the job. Most of his staff had been trained as teachers or diverted from secure jobs in the civil service to work for little pay and with no security in the three small rooms on the top corridor of University College, Earlsfort Terrace, Dublin, the first home of the Irish Folklore Commission. Delargy, who could sell sand to the Arabs or snow to men living in igloos, told us we were the cus-todians of the soul of Ireland, that it was our duty to help gather the fragments of a once great civilisation before it was too late. He had started collection work on a shoestring. In 1935 Taoiseach Éamon de Valera had

Central Station, New York. But it wasn't the end of the story. Delargy was scarcely back in Dublin when a consignment of Ediphone machines addressed to the Irish Folklore Commission arrived with the compliments of the President of the Edison Company. The accompanying note read: 'To a fellow traveller and fisher of men.' These Ediphones were used by the collectors for many years.

Students, scholars, writers, actors, those who wanted some advice or had some information to impart called into the Commission's office from time to time. One of my earliest recollections is of the door of the office opening to admit Micheál Mac Liammóir (1899–1978). He was then in his forties with flashing brown eyes and a classical profile. His coat of green tweed was slung over his shoulders and he spoke beautiful western Irish. Ria Mooney, then one of the Abbey's well known actresses (she had played the part of Rosie Redmond in the first production of Sean O'Casey's *The Plough and the Stars* in 1926) told me that when Micheál was a young man people used stand in the street to watch him go by, so handsome was he. As a child I had been enchanted by his book *Oicheanta Sidhe*, based on four ancient festivals: St Brigid's Eve, May Eve, St John's Eve and Hallowe'en. As a schoolgirl I had saved my pennies to see him act in the Gate Theatre.

In 1940 he had written a modern play, *Where Stars Walk*, which had opened in the presence of President Douglas Hyde. The play was destined to be a theatrical *tour de force*. The curtain rose on a dimly lit stage to a glissando of harp strings plucked by Christopher Casson, while a voice in the shadows chanted from W. B. Yeats's

The Land of Heart's Desire:

> *Until she came into the Land of Faery . . .*
> *And she is still there busied with a dance,*
> *Deep in the dewy shadows of a wood*
> *Or where stars walk upon a mountain top.*

Mac Liammóir had used as leitmotiv an ancient legend about two immortals, Princess Etain and King Midir, reincarnated as servants in a Georgian house on Merrion Square. Now he was in search of material for another play, this one based on the changeling theme, which he would call *Ill Met by Moonlight*.

I hunted out descriptions of charms and spells, how used and when they were most potent, and duly received tickets for the play's opening night in 1946. Micheál was Sebastian Prosper, a French professor of Folklore settled in Connemara, who had as his guests a newly married couple. On May Eve the young bride is abducted by the people of the *Sí* and replaced with a changeling who resembles her physically but has a bitter tongue. The spell is broken when a wreath of flowers sprinkled with the blood of a goat is thrown over the neck of the intruder, who runs out into the night screaming. Almost at once the bride returns, having no idea of where she has been or what has taken place during her absence. *Ill Met by Moonlight* was to prove Micheál Mac Liammóir's most successful play, repeated many times, and was a favourite with amateur theatre groups.

He got into the habit of calling into our rooms in Earlsfort Terrace. He hadn't far to go; he lived just around the corner in Harcourt Terrace with his partner Hilton Edwards, a housekeeper and a couple of cats. The first book I wrote for children was called *Loo the Leprechaun and Báinín the White Cat*. When I gave Micheál a copy he said, 'Ah! I see you are one of us,' which I took to mean that now I was numbered amongst his circle of friends.

He once told how after months of pleading Lady Gregory agreed to introduce him to Yeats. They arranged to meet for lunch in the Standard Hotel in Harcourt Street which had become her Dublin residence. True to form, Micheál arrived late. His profuse apologies were cut short by Yeats: 'You told Lady Gregory you have wanted to meet me for fourteen years,' the poet intoned. 'I see you are exactly fourteen minutes late.' Then his eyes twinkled. 'But you are forgiven, for you are a magnificent actor, Mr Mac Liammóir.'

In the early part of the century informal entertainments known as 'at homes' were popular in Dublin. Oliver St John Gogarty (1878-1957), physician, raconteur, poet, author of *As I Was Going Down Sackville Street* (1937) and student friend of James Joyce, received his friends on Monday nights in his home in Ely Place. Yeats held his evenings on Tuesday, while Sarah Purser, accomplished artist and patron of the arts, was well known for her second Thursdays in Mespil House. George Russell, better known as Æ, was at home on Sundays, while George and Dora Sigerson, who were deeply interested in Irish literature and whose work for Irish political prisoners in English gaols culminated in the Amnesty Act of 1885, welcomed guests on Wednesday nights. This form of entertainment continued to be a feature of Dublin during and after the war years and all comers were welcome. On Saturday nights we went to Delargy's house in Kenilworth Square where he and his charming wife Maud entertained us to tea and scones and the occasional glass of sherry or whiskey. There might even be a bottle of well-matured poteen for men only, brought by a guest from west of the Shannon.

One Hallowe'en the talk turned to ghosts and Micheál told a story about an unearthly experience he had had one night after leaving the theatre. It was lashing rain and he offered to share his taxi with an elderly woman who was standing on the pavement. When they reached her address in Pembroke Road, she invited him in and then went to fetch a book she wished him to have. Idly Micheál examined his surroundings. The room was well furnished in old-fashioned style, the ceiling draped with cobwebs. He felt suddenly chilled and, to distract himself, wrote his name in the dust of the mirror above the mantelpiece. When the old lady returned she handed him a tattered book and then ushered him out without a word.

He felt there was something odd about the meeting and the following day he returned with the excuse of a bunch of flowers. To his astonishment he discovered that the house had been empty for years. He pushed in the creaking door, mounted the carpetless stairs and entered the room. And, yes, there in the dust of the looking-glass was his name even as he had written it the night before. Perhaps the oddest feature of an odd story was that afterwards he could never find the book the old lady had given him nor remember the title. The story was made into a short film, *Return to Glennascaul* (1952), which was produced by Orson Welles and had Micheál and Hilton in it. Whether Orson got the idea from Micheál or the other way round I never found out.

Even today many writers go for inspiration to folklore and the early literature. Seamus Heaney's *Sweeney Astray* (1983) tells of the king of Dal Arie in Ulster who was cursed by a saint, turned into a bird and driven mad for years until his death. It is a version of the medieval *Buile Suibhne* which is based upon a tale that goes back to the seventh century. This looking back into the past was even more true of the forties and fifties when not only Micheál but many more writers were influenced by a motif or plot that could best be found in our archives.

Michael J. Molloy, the folk dramatist who was some-times likened to Synge, came to Dublin a couple of times a year and divided his time between attending the Abbey Theatre, where his plays were produced, and working in our library and archives. He was a quiet, shy bachelor who walked with a limp, lived a solitary life in his smallholding in Milltown, County Galway, and wrote great plays. The theatrical world he created was unequalled, and was dominated by figures from folklore. Yet one of his greatest creations was a simple girl called Sadie in *The Wood of the Whispering* (1953) who is mute by choice. In the entire play she is given one line and that in response to a declaration of love. Michael Molloy told me a moving story about an early romance. He was desperately poor when he wrote the play and much in love with a local girl. He promised her that if the play were a success they would get married. The critics damned it with faint praise, after the first night the public stayed away, and at the end of the week the play was taken off. Soon after, the girl took the boat to England and Michael remained a bachelor to the end of his days.

He is perhaps best remembered for *The King of Friday's Men*, a dark drama with moments of wild humour set in a cottage on the Mayo-Galway border in 1787. Walter Macken, the author and playwright, who was also a brilliant actor from the Taibhdhearc, the all-Irish theatre in Galway, and now long gone 'gentle into that good night', made his name as Bartley Dowd, bully and strong man from Tyrawley. His powerful war-cry, 'Hi for Bartley! Hi for Tyrawley!' nightly shook the walls of the Abbey Theatre as he laid all round him with his shillelagh, driven distracted by his love of Maura Pender, who had been chosen by the landlord Caesar French as his tallywoman.

Until I combed our archives to help Michael Molloy research his play I knew nothing of tallywomen and did not realise that certain Irish landlords practised *droit de seigneur*, taking to their beds the unmarried daughters of their tenants. Some of the squires used the girls they bedded as common whores to be thrown out on the road when the master's eye wandered or his lust was assuaged. Others more kindly treated their bed-mates well, giving them the run of the house, money for clothes and gifts for their parents. If a girl were fortunate, she might find herself married off to a suitable tenant on the estate. The couple would raise any child of the landord's as one of their own and small blame was attached by community or church. Indeed many a one helped her family to modest prosperity by dint of her friendship with the landlord long after she had left his bed. Eilís Dillon in her monumental saga *Across the Bitter Sea* (1973) tells how a girl who has served her time as a tallywoman to a feckless but good-hearted landlord saves her family from starvation during the terrible years of the Famine.

But of all the writers who incorporated Irish folklore into their work, perhaps Frank O'Connor, the twentieth-century master of the short story, is the best known. He sometimes appeared without warning on a Saturday night in Kenilworth Square and would listen attentively while Delargy, who was a gifted raconteur, kept the company enthralled. For a civilised and kindly man, O'Connor had a whiff of brimstone about his person. It was rumoured that he, a married man, had a mistress and son in London. He was yet to meet the American student Harriet Rich whom he would eventually make his wife and with whom he lived happily until his death in 1966 at the relatively early age of sixty-three.

O'Connor, who always wore well-cut tweeds and gold-rimmed glasses, had a wry sense of humour. He had been a revolutionary in his day and told Delargy that he had been educated in an internment camp by his fellow prisoners, many of whom were university students. His experiences during the Civil War provided the raw material for his own favourite story, 'Guests of the Nation'. Two well-meaning and simple British soldiers are taken hostage during the War of Independence, make friends with their captors and are shot as a reprisal for the deaths of two republican prisoners held by the British.

Perhaps the story that best portrays the pride and thirst for revenge among ordinary folk is 'The Majesty of the Law'. Delargy told O'Connor the bones of the story one night in Kenilworth Square in the early thirties. I learnt afterwards how it happened. O'Connor had brought a bottle of whiskey which was duly baptised. Mellowed by a blazing fire and the whiskey, the two got talking of illicit stills, discussing how Mayo had the strongest tradition for poteen-making and how they spilled the first run on the ground there to placate the fairies or Good People – a more prosaic reason being that the first run of poteen can be poisonous. Delargy, who was in fine fettle that night, told of an old poteen-maker who had a row with his neighbour over the quality of the spirits he distilled. Words came to blows and the neighbour took to the law, bringing a charge of assault and battery against his friend. The poteen-maker was fined but refused to pay, opting instead to serve a sentence of seven days in gaol.

O'Connor told Delargy that he had walked home under a starry sky that night, his head filled with pictures of the two old men and their quarrel, and that he had sat up far into the night working on the plot. The result was one of the best short stories Frank O'Connor ever wrote. With rare insight he invokes the atmosphere of the fishing village and the hospitality of Dan Bride when the sergeant comes to arrange for his imprisonment. Even the suspicious old dog comes alive for the reader. Tea and homemade soda bread are provided, as well as a cup of poteen which the guard downs without protest. Finally as they stroll down the lane Dan explains how he, a respectable man, has had to open the head of another old man and why it is that he must go to gaol:

*You see, sergeant, . . . the way it is . . . nothing would
give him more gratification than for me to pay. But
I'll punish him. I'll lie on bare boards for him. I'll
suffer for him, sergeant, so that neither he nor any
of his children after him will be able to raise their
heads for the shame of it.*

And the quarrelsome neighbour, the cause of it all,
scurries into his cottage and closes the door, as old Dan
shakes hands with his neighbours and sets out on the
lonely road to prison.

Gerard Murphy, who was Professor of Irish in UCD, was
a close friend of Delargy and had taken us folklorists
under his wing. He was a delicate man who had been
stricken with tuberculosis, recovered and was devotedly
taken care of by his wife Mary, a strong-minded woman
of great kindness, and a gift to anyone deaf; she could
be heard at the other side of the road. Once a week we
gathered in the drawing-room of their house in Palmerston
Park, sitting on orange boxes – there were never enough
chairs to go round. Following the example of Lady Gregory,
Mary invariably produced a deliciously fruity barmbrack
which we washed down with cups of strong tea. The
Murphys cast their net wide and one might meet at their
home a penniless student who had taken their fancy, a
couple of poets, a novelist, a politician, an up-and-coming
barrister, together with an ex-prisoner Mary had talked
into 'going straight'. But of all the people I met under
their hospitable roof surely the most remarkably different
was James Stephens.

I had been given a copy of his *Irish Fairy Tales* as a

child and later read everything he wrote. He appeared to materialise out of nowhere that spring evening in Palmerston Park, the leprechaun of Irish literature, standing four foot, ten inches tall in his pointed boots, and I thought with awe, this is the author of *The Crock of Gold*; this is the creator of the Grey Woman of Dun Gortin and the Thin Woman of Inish Magrath who knew three questions that puzzled the world. That is until they met the two philosophers who answered correctly what must surely have been the first quiz. After which the ladies married the philosophers in order to be able to pinch them in bed. I was young enough to think it an original and brilliant reason for matrimony.

The talk that night centred on James Joyce, who had died in 1941. Stephens, who rated Joyce second only to Shakespeare, boasted that Joyce and his wife Nora used to visit himself and his wife Cynthia at their house in Kingsbury whenever they were in London and would take afternoon tea in the garden. He claimed that he shared a birthday with Joyce, that they were both born on 2 February 1882. This was disputed after Stephens died; more's the pity. After all, two such originals – and best friends at that – were entitled to claim that they came into the world on the same day. And come to it, what difference does a year make in the sum total of a man's life? But what best I remember about my one and only meeting with James Stephens was that halfway through the evening this little man, almost seventy years of age, retired to a corner of the room and stood on his head for what seemed an age. He swore he regularly exercised in this manner, that it brought fresh blood to his brain and helped him concentrate. I could never manage it myself but thought it a great tip for anyone hoping to get on in life. Alas for fame. How many young people today know who James Stephens is or have read the extraordinary books with which he once dazzled us all?

2
—

CHARMS AND SPELLS

My parents are making a match for me with a man
older than my father. He has a good farm but hasn't
a word to throw to a dog. My brother is bringing a
wife into our place and I am meant to go. I am in
love with a young man who has neither money nor
prospects. What should I do?

I was not much older than the girl who had written that
letter and whose aunt was a part-time collector of folklore. The niece helped the aunt and had become a pen-
friend of mine. When I received the letter I was in the
throes of a passionate and unhappy love affair and much
taken with the story of Deirdre, in *Longes mac nUislenn*,
the great love saga of early literature from the Ulster
cycle. Conor Mac Nessa, the high king of Ireland, decides
to take as his bride, Deirdre, the daughter of his *ollamh*
Fedlimid, who has already fallen in love with Naoise of the
Red Branch Knights. Naoise, accompanied by his two
brothers, elopes with Deirdre to Scotland. For a time all goes
well but the adventure ends badly, as great love stories are

wont to do. Conor lures the runaways back to Ireland, Naoise and his brothers are murdered, the palace at Emain Macha goes up in flames and Deirdre kills herself on a stone.

I was young enough to think the world well lost for love and wrote on those lines to the lovelorn maiden. Whatever the outcome was, we never again heard from either herself or her aunt, and though Delargy may have wondered why, he never for a moment guessed the truth of what had happened. It was only years afterwards that it dawned on me that a 'made' match does not necessarily mean a match made in hell, and that it was not beyond the bounds of possibility that such a couple might end up happy. Peig Sayers (1873–1958), the 'queen of Gaelic storytellers', told me in her old age: 'I never met my husband till the day I married him but it was a lovematch till the day he died.' She remembered him as 'a big handsome man' who never raised his voice to her. Pádraig Ó Guithín, for that was his name, died in his prime and Peig mourned him for the rest of her life. It is interesting that she continued to call herself by her maiden name in the traditional Gaelic manner, a custom that has lately come back. And not a bad idea at that.

I was not long working for the Commission when Delargy discovered that I had a small talent for writing. So for the next couple of years I spent much of my time answering letters from helpers all over the country. Two or three times a year we sent out detailed sets of questions on selected subjects. From 1935 a nucleus of helpers had been built up and by the time I arrived their numbers had grown to around five hundred. They came from all walks of life: teachers, farmers, gardaí, postmistresses, retired bank managers, and the odd solicitor, army officer or Anglo-Irish landowner with a taste for the esoteric. Between 1935 and 1968 fifty major questionnaires were sent out countrywide. Another hundred or so were sent to small numbers of people in localities where particular information was likely to be found. The most regularly recurring topics were the Great Famine of the 1840s, traditional dress, St Brigid's Day and Garland Sunday. The correspondent might labour a month or more over the answers, often asking help of older people. The least the Commission could do was to keep in touch. Once a year we sent out a bulletin, run off on an old-fashioned Gestetner machine, telling how the work was progressing and including interesting snippets of lore that our helpers might like to read.

Occasionally someone would write in for a small favour: the purchase of a special brand of tobacco or snuff which could be got only in Fox's tobacconists in Dublin, or for a length of silk or velvet in a particular shade unavailable in the local drapers. Once I was asked to buy a bridal gown in Switzers store in Grafton Street; I was given the measurements and later invited to the wedding, an invitation I was forced to decline. I heard afterwards that the gown was the talk of the parish. People were punctilious about defraying the cost of their purchases, often urging me to buy something for myself with any extra change or suggesting that the money be used to have a Mass said or a candle lit. I reckon that over the years I must have lit dozens of candles for the intentions of people I was fated never to meet. If an informant died we offered our sympathy. The relatives usually wrote back and this often led to an exchange of

of Denmark, remarked, 'There are more things in heaven and earth, Horatio, than are dreamt of in your philosophy.'

The people of the *Sí* could be malignant if interfered with, and people did their best to propitiate these unearthly beings: leaving unsalted food outside the door at night, casting a scrap of food on the ground if someone sneezed, spilling milk and, as we have already noted, the first run of poteen for their use. Recently I heard on the news how a farmer objected because the ESB were uprooting a fairy thorn tree on his land. Cattle and even human beings (especially children and young brides) were said to be 'taken away by the fairies'. One old woman from a remote corner of Donegal wrote to tell us how her granddaughter had been abducted by the fairies on the night of her wedding, even sending me a photograph of the girl in all her finery. That story was to have a sequel; many years later I came face to face with the 'abducted bride' but that was in another country. The wench had eloped with a company of travelling actors who were passing through the village. When we met she was on her fifth (and very wealthy) husband and had a Jaguar car and a pet pug.

Stories of changelings were common in Ireland, as well as in many other parts of western Europe. An old man in Galway wrote that his grandfather had encountered a changeling when he was asked by neighbours to take care of their baby while they went to the horse fair in Ballinasloe. The child, they confessed, had lately become peevish and was causing them no end of trouble; so, to amuse the infant, the man brought along his fiddle to play a few tunes. He had barely drawn his bow when the child jumped out of the cradle shouting, 'You're out of tune!'

The fiddler, a man of few words, took up a sod of turf with the tongs to redden his pipe, at which the child ran screeching out the door. He realised that he was dealing with one of the fairy folk, who are scared of iron and fire. 'Send the stolen child back,' he shouted after the runaway, and sure enough a little while later the real baby came toddling into the kitchen.

This story would no doubt find a simple rational explanation today. An illness or even a teething problem can cause a change in a normally good-tempered child; it is easy to see how, when the child spontaneously re-covered, the belief should have become established that a switch had been made and that the changeling had gone back to its own.

Belief in fairies continued in Ireland up to recent times. It flourished here longer than anywhere else and to an unusual degree, owing to the imaginative powers of the Irish and to the fact that in Irish folk belief there is little difference between the kingdom of the dead and the fairy world. Fairies were said to resemble human beings and each human had a fairy double, a kind of guardian angel. It was commonly held that they were fallen angels, part of the heavenly host who rebelled with Lucifer and were cast out of heaven. Halfway between heaven and hell they had second thoughts, repented and were stopped in their tracks where they remained, earthbound but invisible. Having lost their places in heaven they were keen to regain them. One story tells how fairies accosted a priest out at night on a sick call and asked him if they would ever gain salvation. When he could give them no hope, they raised such lamentations that they could be heard over half the country. To spite the priest they lamed his horse, and, but for the fact that he was carrying the holy oils, would have destroyed him entirely.

Waking the dead with clay pipes, snuff, porter, whiskey, food and drink was still common in the Ireland of the forties and fifties; wake games that went back to pagan times were still played. Young people took advantage of the general air of freedom to do their courting and, as the saying went: 'Many's the match was made at a wake.' A carpenter's widow wrote to say that she had buried her husband's hammer in his coffin so that he could use it to knock on the gates of heaven. Money was put into the mouth of the corpse to pay the ferryman to take it across the Styx, the river of death. Food and drink were buried with the dead, a custom that continued to be observed until quite recent times. Twenty years ago a grave in County Limerick was opened in error. Before filling it in again, the gravediggers sprinkled a loaf with holy water and placed it in the hole with the explanation that the sleep of those who were buried in the spot had been broken. They had been brought back by mistake and would need food for the return journey.

Keening women who could raise a lament, extolling the virtues of the deceased, were warmly welcomed at a wake. One woman from Bantry travelled all over County Cork to raise the keen. Her proud boast was that she never accepted a penny in payment, though she might be persuaded to take a ham, a fowl or a bottle of port, or if nothing else was on offer, the rosary of the deceased. If a wife had the gift of words, she might make the lament herself, extemporising as she went along.

3

THE LAST OF THE GREAT LOVE POEMS

One of the best-known love poems in the Irish language is '*Caoineadh Airt Uí Laoghaire*' ('The Lament for Art O'Leary'). Scion of one of the last noble Catholic families to survive in the Ireland of the eighteenth century, Art O'Leary was a landowner of Iveleary in west Cork. It was there, in wild and lovely Céim an Fhiaidh, the Pass of the Deer, that I first heard the lament. The mile-long pass that once separated the O'Leary lands from the O'Sullivan runs through the purple-tipped mountains on the borders of Cork and Kerry. I was a schoolgirl, attending the Irish college, and had gone for a walk that took me past Gougane Barra and on into the pass. I can still see the woman, dressed in homespun, who called me from her cottage door with a cup of milk. She had hair the colour of the sloes that grew in profusion along the road, hazel eyes shaded by incredible lashes and a strawberry mark on one cheek that seemed to enhance rather than diminish her looks. 'Eibhlín Dubh bore such a mark on her neck,' she said and I looked at her in puzzlement, wondering who on earth Eibhlín Dubh was. Masses of rock rising hundreds of feet in the air cast an air of melancholy grandeur over the place and though the evening air was warm I was shivering with cold. 'Uibh-Laoghaire still echoes to the death agony of Art Ó Laoghaire,' the woman said. 'His name will live forever because of the lament his wife made.' She invited me into the kitchen and we sat at a table scrubbed to a milky whiteness while she told me the story that has passed into the folklore of the district.

Art O'Leary had seen service as captain of the Hungarian hussars under Empress Maria Theresa of Austria. He later returned to Ireland and married the beautiful Eibhlín Dubh – Dark Eileen, an aunt of Daniel O'Connell, the man who, a little over half a century later, would secure Catholic Emancipation. The year was 1773 and the infamous Penal Laws, though largely inactive, were still in force. Among many other injustices, these laws forbade a Catholic's owning a horse worth more than £5, the paltry sum Abraham Morris, the high-sheriff of the Macroom district, offered O'Leary for his splendid mare. The offer was refused with scorn and a quarrel with Morris ensued; O'Leary was outlawed but his vow to kill Morris was never fulfilled because he perished in an ambush set up by Morris's men near Carriganima. The riderless horse made its way back to Raleigh House outside Macroom where Eibhlín Dubh was waiting. When she saw the blood-spattered saddle she knew her husband was dead and composed the beautiful elegy. O'Leary was buried in Kilcrea Abbey where a stone with an inscription marks his last resting place:

Lo! Art O'Leary, generous, handsome, brave,
Slain in his youth, lies in this humble grave.

On that day long ago a simple countrywoman recited all thirty-six verses of Eibhlín Dubh's lament for her husband. I can still hear the soft lilting Cork voice as she spoke the opening line, '*Mo ghrá go daingean! Lá dá bhfaca thú...*' ('My love forever, the day I first saw you...') and the change of voice as verse followed heartbreaking verse: the tender praise of their married life, the pride in Art's noble deeds, the tongue-lashing with which she curses his killers. Finally the voice seemed to steady as she tells the mourners to cease their tears while Art is being laid in his grave, '*ag iompair cré agus cloch*'. I still think the '*Caoineadh*' is one of the great love poems of all time.

Folk memory can be very tenacious. Seán O'Sullivan told me once how a fisherman in Dunquin could remember the lament half a century after he had heard it for the first and only time. A group of fishermen were caught in a storm one night and were forced to seek shelter in the lee of the Tiaracht Rock beyond the Blasket Islands. They passed the night telling stories and one man from Iveragh recited the '*Caoineadh*' which the fisherman from Dunquin committed to memory. He said he would carry the remembrance of that night to his grave: the storm-swept sky, the howling gale, the sea crashing on the rocks, and above and beyond it all the beauty and rhythm of the words of the last of the great Irish laments.

Another fascinating encounter was my meeting with the Tailor and Ansty. They were a married couple who lived in a small house standing on the brow of a hill on the road up from Gougane Barra. They had an acre of land, hens, geese and a cow which was their most treasured possession, and were passing rich on the Tailor's old-age pension of ten shillings a week. Gougane Barra is an enchanting wooded spot and in the small graveyard the famous couple take their last sleep under a beautiful headstone designed by Seamus Murphy, the Cork sculptor. Nearby are the remains of the oratory and the lake where St Finbarr founded his hermitage before following the course of the river Lee to the marshes where the city of Cork now stands.

Tailors were popular storytellers and bearers of traditions, possibly because they moved from village to village and house to house plying their trade. They would spend a couple of weeks staying in the most comfortable house in the district making clothes for all in the parish. Their first job was 'whipping the cat', taking a door off the hinges and setting it on a matting of straw. Here they sat cross-legged, measuring, cutting out cloth, sewing up suits for men and boys, and cloaks for women. When the day's work was done, people for miles around would come visiting to relay the gossip of the townland and hear tales of the outside world. Because of their acquaintance with many parishes and their capacity for picking up stories and information wherever they went, they were considered wise and knowledgeable men.

The tailor of Gougane Barra was in his seventies when I first laid eyes on him, a small man with a merry roguish face and the agility of a goat, despite his withered leg. He spoke beautiful Irish, as did the people of Ballingeary and the surrounding district. He had long since given up his tailoring, his favourite saying being: '*Glac bog an saol and glacfaidh an saol bog thú*', which roughly translates as: 'Take life easy and life will take you easy too.' He had travelled all over Ireland and as far afield as Scotland but was now content to remain at home while the world came to his door. Around his fire you might meet Frank O'Connor, Father Tim Traynor from the Star of the Sea parish in Sandymount, Dublin, Nancy McCarthy, a well known chemist from Cork, and Eric Cross, who was to write *The Tailor and Ansty* (1942) (with such disastrous results), as well as neighbours who called in for the nightly crack. I met Ansty at Mass in Gougane Barra and admired her hooded cloak made of fine black broadcloth, faced with braid and lined with satin. At one time the hooded cloak was the outer garment of women all over the country but times had changed and west Cork was one of the last places where it was worn. Ansty, whose full name was Anastasia, had a sharp tongue and knew how to keep the Tailor's vivid imagination in check, though she enjoyed his stories as well as the next, and indeed if he went astray in their telling would soon put him right. They divided the work of the house and the care of the acre of ground fairly, and kept a watchful eye on the cow.

Ansty cleaned, baked the bread, fed the poultry, collected the eggs and sold the produce in the local shop where she bought flour, tea, sugar, soap and Jacobs biscuits, of which she was inordinately fond. The Tailor cooked the dinner and once a week 'made the churn', a strenuous job even for a younger and fitter man. He used an old-fashioned dash-churn, working the plunger up and down until the cream cracked and the butter formed. Any visitor to the house was expected to take a hand. It was the custom and said to bring good luck. The cow, their pride and joy, was the cornerstone of their economy and produced milk in abundance. She calved once a year and was responsible for the golden butter and cream they used. The surplus was sold or exchanged for goods. Not only that but she gave them manure, which helped the growth of vegetables on their plot; for, as the Tailor said, 'The land needs all you can give it. It is as rare as good sense and like commonsense cannot be bought.'

The Tailor admired my buckled shoes and told me that when he was a young lad people went barefoot unless on their way to Mass. 'At that time there was no left or right boot. You changed your footwear, putting the left on the right and vice versa, and never got corn or welt.' While Ansty plied me with strong tea, homemade bread and butter, freshly made, and honey from the hive, the Tailor fed Carlo the dog and Kitty the cat, boasting that they understood every word he said. He gave it as gospel that at one time every living creature had the power of speech and told me a well known folktale to prove his point:

The cockroach was known as the 'devil's coach-horse' because it had betrayed the Holy Family fleeing from Herod's soldiers into Egypt. Heaven had worked a miracle, ripening corn in one night, so that when Herod's soldiers came in pursuit, the farmer could truthfully say that the Holy Family had passed that way on the day he was planting the corn. The

> *soldiers grumbled that, judging by the harvest,*
> *months must have elapsed since that sowing but the*
> *cockroach stuck up his head calling out: 'Inné! Inné!'*
> *('Yesterday! Yesterday!') and the soldiers went in hot*
> *pursuit. And heaven was so angered that, as a*
> *punishment, from that day to this, insects and even*
> *animals have lost the power of speech.*

The Tailor shook his head sadly at his peroration.

It is fifty years and more since Eric Cross wrote the story of the Tailor and Ansty. I read it again recently and was once more charmed by its innocence and simplicity, and the evidence of the welcome the old pair gave to all comers. The book is a homage to times long past. And yet in 1942 the Censorship Board banned this story as being 'in its general tendency indecent'. This caused an uproar in the Senate. The man who sprang to its defence was a Protestant landlord, Sir John Keane, who tabled a motion in the House condemning the Board. After the banning and bad publicity, the Tailor and Ansty were ostracised. Frank O'Connor tells a story that might have come out of the Inquisition. Seemingly, not long after the book had been banned, three priests arrived at the couple's door and forced the old man to burn his copy at the fire he was tending. After that a friendly guard cycled out from Ballingeary a couple of times a week to make sure that the old couple were safe and to ward off hooligans. When the Tailor's friends, O'Connor and Father Traynor, came down from Dublin, they found Ansty hysterical and the Tailor comforting her with the words: '*Tóg bog é, a chailín!* (Take it easy, girl!) At our age there is little the world can do.' It took ten years for the censorship law to be relaxed and, wonder of wonders, one of the first books discovered not to be obscene after all was the very one that had caused such heartache and pain and that had probably hastened the deaths of two simple and gentle old folk.

a book we would jointly write. It was bound to be a success. We would give back to the children of Ireland the stories that had been collected years before. However, when I approached Delargy with the idea, it was not well received. I was reminded that the Commission's task was to collect and collate the folklore of Ireland before it was too late. Everything else must take second place.

I was disappointed but whenever I got the chance I browsed through the stories, and fascinating reading they made. During the school year 1937–38, children in the twenty-six counties took part in a scheme to collect the folklore of their native districts. They were excused homework and given a set of questions on various topics by their teachers. The idea was that they should question grandparents and elderly neighbours and write down the answers in specially provided notebooks. The inspiration came from Delargy and had the support of the Department of Education. As an exercise it had the merits of being both imaginative and novel. The children were delighted with anything that freed them of hated homework and they enjoyed questioning their elders. Relations and neighbours in turn were happy to tell stories of their young days and share the folklore and history of their neighbourhood. All this resulted in a fine body of material on subjects as disparate as tales and legends of the Irish countryside, rhymes and riddles, children's games, farming, fishing, crafts, holy wells, festivals, wakes and weddings and, of course, the people of the Other World.

A favourite story had to do with the Hag of Beare, said to be the oldest and wisest woman in Ireland. She could remember back to the Ice Age. Then there was the Earl of Desmond, who rode the waters of Lough Gur in County Limerick, and the O'Donoghue of the Glens, who galloped over the Lakes of Killarney. But the best-known figure in Irish folklore was undoubtedly the Banshee (*bean sí* – fairy woman). There wasn't a person in town or country who had not heard or seen the banshee. She was known as the messenger of death, a weird and ghostly presence who might be seen cowering under a tree or perched on top of a house, combing her hair while crying and keening. She wore a long dark cloak and her feet were never seen. Woe betide anyone at whom she happened to fling her comb; should it find its mark, that person was doomed soon to die.

Another story popular with the children told of a man who discovered a banshee's comb in a field. Came midnight and he heard wailing around the house. He opened the window and held the comb out with the tongs. As he did so, a ghostly hand reached out leaving him half the tongs and the scorched mark of five fingers.

Not everyone could boast a banshee in the family; she was a bit of a snob. It was said that she haunted only the best families, with offspring born on the right side of the blanket. Piaras Feiritéar, the seventeenth-century Kerry poet, disparaged the merchants of Dingle when they claimed to have heard the wailing: 'They need not fear that the banshee would raise a lament for them,' he said scathingly. 'The cry they heard was for one of the noble Fitzgeralds.'

She was said to follow not only aristocratic Normans but also people of artistic merit, especially those possessing the gift of music. Families whose names began with O or Mac could also claim her attention. One of the popular jingles that children playing skipping games turned the ropes to was:

By Mac and O, you'll surely know
True Irishmen, they say
But if they lack both O and Mac
No Irishmen are they.

If a seriously ill person heard the cry of the banshee, it was a sign that their end was near. The tradition of the banshee spread even to the New World, carried across the Atlantic by emigrants from the Ireland of the nineteenth and early twentieth centuries, and there too her appearance was considered something of a status symbol by the selected family.

Legends of death messengers can be traced back to pre-Christian Ireland. In the '*Táin Bó Cuailgne*' ('The Cattle Raid of Cooley'), one of the oldest stories in ancient Irish literature, Cuchulain holds the Pass of Ulster against the army of Maeve, Queen of Connacht, in a series of single-handed encounters. When he sets out on his final fateful battle he meets a beautiful woman washing severed limbs and bloodstained clothes at Átha na Foraire on the plains of Emain Macha. Cathfad, his druid, warns him that the girl is the banshee and that slaughter will follow him but Cuchulain refuses to turn back in spite of the pleas of his mother Dechtire and his wife Emer. A thousand years later the banshee, in the form of the fairy queen, Aoibheall, appears to Brian Boru on the eve of the Battle of Clontarf (1014) to forewarn him that he will be killed on the morrow, but the high king, like all great heroes, believes that whatever is fated will come to pass.

Sixty years have elapsed since the Schools Collection was carried out. Many of those who contributed have gone *ar shlí na fírinne* (the way of truth). Any who are still alive or any of their families can be assured of a warm welcome in the Department of Irish Folklore at University College Dublin. In the thousand and more bound volumes that make up the Schools Collection they may read the stories and the details of traditions and history that their grandparents and neighbours gave so generously to those bright-eyed and inquisitive youngsters all those years ago.

5

AT THE FOOT OF THE RAINBOW

In April 1992 Euro Disney opened its gates to the public
in Paris and a cheer went up as Mickey and Minnie Mouse
emerged. In Disneyland children can still enjoy the magic
of Snow White and the Seven Dwarfs, of Pinocchio and
the rest of the screen fairytales, but above all the myth
of Walt Disney as everybody's favourite uncle.

The Second World War was over, life was returning to
normal and Ireland was emerging from her self-imposed
isolation when, in the summer of 1946, word reached us
via the Department of External Affairs (now the Department of Foreign Affairs) that Walt Disney was coming
to Dublin and that his first port of call would be the
offices of the Irish Folklore Commission. It was his
intention to make a film dealing with Irish fairy folk.
Delargy was enthusiastic, and manuscripts and volumes
were taken down from shelves, dusted and made ready
for Disney's inspection. He was one of the first of the
post-war visitors who would land upon our shores, and
the excitement in the air was palpable. Students huddled
in groups in the main hall of University College, waiting

to see the man whose films had delighted their childhood; staff lingered at the doors of empty lecture rooms lest they miss the sight of the great animator, and the usual cluster of autograph hunters gathered at the main door. A fleet of cars drew up on the terrace, a press of photographers leaped forward, cameras poised, as a dark man with a moustache and wearing a soberly cut grey suit was hustled inside. The head porter, a man with a proper sense of his own importance, took it upon himself to escort the American party up to the top corridor of the College, where our offices were situated. John Battle, Disney's right-hand man, rooted in his pocket to tip the porter and came up with the biggest coin he could find – a penny piece. The porter was deeply insulted. It took all Delargy's powers of persuasion to placate him and to get him to accept a tip of a pound note (a substantial sum in those days) sweetened by a signed portrait of Disney himself.

Revisionism is a darlin' word, as Joxer Daly might have said. It simply means writing history from a different point of view or, in the case of a well known person gone to higher judgement, disinterring their frailities for our delectation. The dead have no defence; they cannot explain nor threaten a libel action. Walt Disney, who died in 1962, has lately been discredited as a heavy drinker, an unpaid FBI agent during the McCarthy era and a tyrant who ran his celluloid empire as a sweatshop. The fact that he was a genius who had a miserable upbringing counts for nothing. The mid-west farmer he called father was a Bible-belt fundamentalist, a brutal bully given to whiskey, poker and wild women. He employed Walt as a farm labourer, thrashing him unmercifully as payment for his labours. When Walt tried to enlist in the American forces, he was devastated when no birth certificate could be found for him. His search for an identity was to become a life's quest, ending up in the make-believe world of Hollywood. It is said that the FBI promised to discover the truth about his parentage in return for his help.

Looking back to what might be called an era of either innocence or ignorance, I remember the creator of Mickey Mouse as a soft-spoken, gentle person, with sad eyes but a great sense of humour. Delargy, like the Department of External Affairs, was dismayed that he had come to Ireland with the intention of making a film about lep-rechauns. For some reason I could never fathom, lep-rechauns have always had a bad press.

Following the wishes of our director, we tried to interest Disney in one or other of the great heroic sagas: the '*Táin*' or 'The Well at the World's End', where the hero undertakes twelve impossible tasks before bedtime and then claims the hand of the princess in marriage. There was the story of Deirdre, Ireland's answer to Helen of Troy, or 'The Pursuit of Diarmaid and Gráinne', which was made into a play in Irish by Micheál Mac Liammóir. We told him of the story of the children of Lir who, enchanted by a wicked stepmother, were forced to spend nine hundred years in the shape of swans, dividing their time between Derravaragh Lake in County Westmeath, the stormy sea of Moyle between Antrim and Scotland, and the black and bitter waters of Erris off the coast of County Mayo. But no; nothing but leprechauns would do the man who had set his heart on meeting one and had travelled across the Atlantic in the hope that his wish might come true.

Mind you, I had a certain fellow-feeling with Disney. I have always liked leprechauns, and the first book for children I wrote featured the adventures of a particularly clever member of that tribe. Leprechauns have been around these parts for thousands of years. They are reputed to have been kin to the shadowy *Tuatha De Danann*, whose magic was no match for the iron weapons of the belligerent Celts when they first came to settle here. In the main, leprechauns have always been hardworking creatures, shoemakers by trade, lending a splash of colour to the countryside with their green jackets, red caps and white owl's feathers. Furthermore, they are associated with that marvel of nature, the rainbow, beneath whose foot they hide their crocks of gold.

Why someone did not sell Disney the idea of making a film about our earliest leprechaun I shall never understand. It would have made a marvellous picture. The adventure would take too long to tell in detail here; suffice it to say that the story describes how Eisirt, poet to the king of the leprechauns, comes on a visit to Ireland. He finds himself in the banqueting hall at Emain Macha, where he is mocked for his size, almost drowned in a beaker of wine, half-smothered in a pot of porridge and finally befriended by Aed, the Irish king's jester, whom he invites home. The story ends on a splendid note:

Aed was treated nobly in the kingdom of the leprechauns and after that he went back to the palace of Emain Macha and wrote down in golden ink in

the Annals of Ulster *the story of how Eisirt came to
Ireland and all he could remember of Mag Faithlenn,
which lies off the west coast of Ireland and is the
true home of the dwarves.*

Walt Disney did not linger long in Dublin but set off,
accompanied by Delargy, on a tour of the country. The
weather turned out to be typically Irish, sunshine and rain
– the smile and the tear, as Tom Moore, the maker of
sentimental verse, has described our climate. Undoubtedly
Disney's heart was gladdened by the magnificent rainbows
they saw stretching across the sky on their travels,
touching the Maamturk mountains in Connemara and
Carrantuohill in the deep south. He remained hopeful that
he would encounter fairy folk – or at least someone who
knew of their whereabouts. Delargy introduced him to an
old man who had a story for every day of the year and
was reputed to have been caught up in the *sí gaoithe* –
the fairy winds. Disney was impressed by this record of
supernatural achievement and opened up the conversation with the query: 'Tell me, sir, did you ever meet a
leprechaun?' Quick as lightning came the riposte: 'Begod
then if I didn't see a leprechaun, Mr Disney, I saw his
traces.' And that was as near to leprechauns as Walt
Disney was likely to get.

What was filmed in the end was a rather pallid little
story called *Darby O'Gill and the Little People*, redeemed
only by the acting of Jimmy O'Dea as Brian, king of the
leprechauns. Jimmy was Ireland's greatest comedian, a
man who could wring tears of laughter from a stone. The
film was premièred in Dublin and was followed by a

banquet hosted by the Lord Mayor of Dublin and the city fathers in the Mansion House. We humble members of staff of the Irish Folklore Commission mingled with the *crème de la crème* of the city: politicians, bishops, businessmen, actors, producers and others with an overweening sense of their own importance.

It turned out to be the best and the worst night of my life. After the austerity of the post-war years, the feast of the creamy soup, the prawn cocktails, the Beef Wellington, the Crêpes Suzettes and chocolate soufflés, followed by Irish coffee, made me feel as if I were taking part in a Hollywood orgy. But it was the champagne that was to prove my Waterloo. True, I had tasted that wine fleetingly and in small sips at a couple of weddings I had attended, but never in such quantities as to form a lasting impression. Some ill-advised person told me it was possible to drink any amount of the stuff with no unpleasant effects. So I, whose usual tipple was a modest glass of sherry, knocked back all the champagne that was on offer (and I have to admit that on the night in question it flowed like water). I even took a bottle of the fizz home with me, where I fell into bed without drinking the statutory gallon of water and woke in the early hours with the most dreadful hangover I have ever experienced. That night made me chary of one of life's fine pleasures.

Before he left Ireland, Walt Disney gave each of the staff of the Commission a small gift: a scarf, a tiepin, a silver ring stamped with the figure of Mickey Mouse. Hesitantly I offered Disney a copy of the book for children I had written, called *Loo the Leprechaun and Báinín the White Cat.* To my surprise he liked it and offered me a job as scriptwriter in his studios in Hollywood, but Delargy said that the work I was doing in Ireland was more important, and anyhow Los Angeles was unknown country at that time and far away.

I was always sorry I didn't get to know Walt Disney better. Perhaps his passion for leprechauns was bound up in the belief that happiness can be found at the end of the rainbow and that in the land of fairy it doesn't matter who your parents were or, indeed, if you ever knew them. Years later Jack Kinney, Walt Disney's chief animator, on a visit to Dublin, picked out in Eason's bookshop *The Search for the Tinker Chief*, another children's book I had written. (This was in the days when the word 'tinker' referred to the age-old tinsmith's craft of the travelling people, before it became the pejorative term it is today.) Kinney liked the book, met me and my publisher, then flew off to Hollywood where Disney took an option on the book while Kinney prepared storyline and drawings. Sadly, within a year he died of a heart attack and with him the dream of that film. It seemed I was not fated after all to make my name and fortune with the Disney Studios.

6

CLIMBING CROAGH PATRICK

Every year on the last Sunday of July, known as Garland Sunday, thousands of people climb the 'Reek', as Croagh Patrick in County Mayo is familiarly known. The pilgrimage is to honour Ireland's national apostle, St Patrick. In his *Confessio* Patrick tells us how he was captured by raiders and taken as a slave to Ireland. He escaped and spent some years in Gaul, where he was ordained and later consecrated bishop, with which office he returned to Ireland. He was not the first missionary to reach our shores. Before his time there were already small communities of Christians. There are differences of opinion as to the date of his actual arrival but it almost certainly occurred between 430 and 435.

Even today the ascent of Croagh Patrick is a breathtaking experience. Most of the time the peaks are shrouded in mist but on a clear day you can see for ever. To the west the wide Atlantic rolls ceaselessly; northwards across the bay the cliffs of Achill are starkly outlined. To the south is the vast and desolate country of Mayo and Connemara, and in contrast a great plain fans out to the east incorporating the counties of Roscommon and Galway, and the banks of the Shannon.

According to tradition, it was on this wild and lonely height that St Patrick fasted for forty days and forty nights and was visited first by a horde of demons and then by myriad white birds. The insistent Patrick exacted a promise from heaven that he would be there at the final judgement to see that justice be done to his adopted Irish and that due allowance be made for their sins and omissions. He made a further compact with heaven that the countless number of birds hovering around the mountain would equal the number of Irish souls to be saved on the Last Day. Little wonder that we have cause to be grateful to Patrick or that all over the world the people of the Irish diaspora make it their business to see that his feast is celebrated in proper style.

What is startling about this climb is that it has been taking place for thousands of years. For the ascent is not really a Christian survival at all but has its roots deep in prehistory. Aeons ago pilgrims climbed the mountain to honour Lugh, the god of the pagan Celts. Lughnasa, one of the four quarterly feasts of the old Irish year, marked the beginning of the harvest.

In 1942 the Commission issued a questionnaire about Garland Sunday and got an overwhelming response. Various accounts described how people celebrated the beginning of the harvest by making trips to hills, mountains and lakes on either the last Sunday of July or the first Sunday of August. They picked bilberries and wild fruit, ate the first of the new potatoes and whatever other food they had brought along, drank homemade wine and poteen, told stories and danced the night away to the music of the fiddle, tin whistle, mouth organ and accordion. The Lughnasa festival was known not only as Garland Sunday but also as Whort Sunday, Bilberry Sunday, Fraughan Sunday, Harvest Sunday, *Domhnach Deireannach an tSamraidh* (the last Sunday of summer), Pattern Sunday and, along the Irish-speaking western seaboard, *Domhnach Chrom Dubh* (Black Crom's Sunday), from the name of an idol worshipped in Connacht.

The term Lammas came in with the Scots and English settlers but never passed into the Gaelic speech. Lammas Day, celebrated on 1 August, was known to the native Irish as 'Lewy's Fair', a corruption of the Irish word *Lugh*. Kuno Meyer, the noted Irish scholar, described the feast:

Lammas Day makes known its dues
In each distant year,
Testing every favourite fruit
Food of herbs at Lughnasa.

Máire MacNeill, whose post as secretary of the Irish Folklore Commission I took over in 1949 when she left to marry the Irish-American academic Jack Sweeney and went to live in Boston, had a lifelong fascination with the feast of Lughnasa. Thirteen years after her marriage she published the monumental *Festival of Lughnasa*, in which a panorama of customs, beliefs and traditions is unfolded. I discovered to my great delight that the pagan god Lugh is associated with leprechauns and is known as the patron of shoemakers; and also that little men can sometimes be glimpsed on the hills of Ben Scardaun, County Meath.

One of the oldest stories in the literature has to do with Lughnasa and proves that the pagan Irish believed in reincarnation or the transmigration of souls. The story of Midir and Etain was first written down from oral sources in the *Lebor na hUidre* (The Book of the Dun Cow) in the great monastery of Clonmacnoise about the year 1100. It passed again into oral tradition and is particularly associated with County Longford at a place called Ardagh Hill, or to use its ancient name, Brí Leith, one of the most famous fairy seats in Ireland.

Brí Leith was the home of a giant called King Midas, a corruption of King Midir of the *Sí*. His wife Etain was changed into a crimson fly by a jealous rival. A magic wind carried the fly to Tara where it fell into a goblet of wine and was swallowed by a young bride eating her supper. Nine months later the girl gave birth to a daughter, whom she called Etain. Years later the high king of Ireland made Etain his queen. Now at the beginning of Lughnasa when the harvest was gathered, Midir of the *Sí* came to Tara in search of his lost love. He challenged the high king to a game of chess, won the game and carried his queen back to the fairy mound of Brí Leith.

This was the story that Micheál Mac Liammóir used as the theme of his play *Where Stars Walk*. Years later Brian Friel would incorporate the traditions and stories surrounding the festival in his play *Dancing at Lughnasa*. Off-stage, bonfires are lit on the mountain and there are sounds of people making merry. In the Donegal farmhouse tensions mount as the story unfolds, with the four sisters reacting in different ways to the spirit of the festival. They finally give vent to their feelings in a frenzy of dancing around the kitchen floor.

It is no exaggeration to say that the Irish have always loved dancing and it is not to be wondered at that in our own times *Riverdance* brought people to their feet in a passion of applause when it was first performed as a ten-minute Eurovision 'filler' at the Gaiety Theatre in 1995. W. B. Yeats so grips our imagination with his version of the fourteenth-century poem 'Icham of Irlaunde' that President Mary Robinson felt impelled to use it in her inaugural speech:

> *'I am of Ireland,*
> *And the Holy Land of Ireland,*
> *And time runs on,' cried she.*
> *'Come out of charity,*
> *Come dance with me in Ireland.'*

The love that ordinary folk had for dancing in pre-Famine Ireland is shown in an account left us by Lord George Hill, who owned property in Donegal. He describes his tenants moving a cabin from one site to another:

> *They hired a fiddler upon which engagement all the neighbours joyously assembled and carried in an incredibly short time the stones and timber upon their backs to the new site, men, women and children alternately dancing and working while daylight lasted, at the termination of which they adjourned to a nearby dwelling where they finished the night, prolonging the dance to the dawn of day.*

A good travel writer can bring to life a scene he has witnessed, so vividly that we might suppose we had taken part in the journey. H. D. Inglis, in his book *Ireland in 1834*, relates how on *Domhnach Chrom Dubh*, as the Lughnasa festival was known in the Joyce country of Mamturk, County Galway, he made his way to a gathering on the heights:

> *Far up the winding road for miles we could see the women in their red petticoats and the men in their bawneens. Soon we were overtaken by a merry crowd of boys and girls dancing along, led by a piper, playing a jig. We reached the summit where the pattern was at its height; tents, people seated on the grass, others doing the rounds of the holy well, others still dancing around a bonfire, singing the while. The innkeeper who accompanied me whispered that soon there would be a faction fight and we had not long to wait. Out of various tents sallied boys flourishing shillelaghs. After a scrimmage which lasted perhaps ten minutes and in which there were some broken skulls but none badly injured, the Joyces remained masters of the field. The women took no part in the fight.*

The writer describes the descent at the end of the day with the evening sun flaming down the cleft and gilding the slopes:

> *A long line of pilgrims and horses stretching for miles down the length of the defile, the mountain*

notes of the pipes, feet jigging in time, the occasional burst of voices and the lowing of the cattle filling all the hollows of the the hills. It was quite dark when we reached Maam.

7
—

FAREWELL TO THE PIPER

Of all the people I worked with, probably Máire MacNeill influenced me most. She was a tall slim blonde who wore her hair in a French pleat and invariably dressed in black. She was the daughter of Eoin MacNeill, co-founder of the Gaelic League and the Irish Volunteers, Professor of Early Irish History at UCD. Máire had many stories of her early years on Inis Mór in the Aran Islands when her father was sentenced to life imprisonment after the 1916 Rising. She was a scholar and, though I was years younger and not a scholar at all, she treated me as an equal and a friend. I had the pleasure of dancing at her wedding.

After her husband retired as curator and librarian at Harvard, they settled at Corofin, County Clare, where she became interested in Máire Rua O'Brien (née Mahon), the seventeenth-century chatelaine of Leamaneh Castle near Inchiquin. I was also keenly interested in Máire Rua (possibly because her maiden name was the same as my own) and I used her story as the introduction to my novel of Peg Woffington's life, *A Time to Love*. She was so celebrated that after her death she became the best-known character in Clare folklore. If she were alive today she would undoubtedly find her way into the glossy magazines, become a television personality and write a bestseller. She was an extremely beautiful, strong-minded redhead who, according to folklore, was married twenty-five times. (In actual fact she managed only three husbands.)

She was born in Bunratty Castle, her mother's old home, and was the niece of Donough O'Brien, fourth Earl of Thomond, known as the Great Earl, who kept state at the castle. He was the most important and the wealthiest man in north Munster. Máire Rua's first marriage was made for dynastic reasons; her second, to Conor O'Brien, was a love match. He was outlawed and killed by the Cromwellians and his castle and lands were confiscated. In a desperate attempt to save the estate, Máire Rua made a dramatic drive in a coach and four, dressed in blue and silver, to the garrison in Limerick, where she successfully seduced the much-feared Cromwellian general, Sir Henry Ireton. In return for her favours he granted her a free pardon, secured her castle and lands and married her off to one of his officers. According to the stories of the district, Máire Rua soon grew tired of the rough Cromwellian and pushed him out of a high window to his death on the cobbles below. She is further said to have kept among her attendants twelve youths dressed as women to be on hand to pleasure her. She haunts Toonagh Woods, where she met her death out riding when her long red hair caught in the branch of a tree and strangled her.

Another favourite colleague of mine from the early days was Séamus Ennis, *ard rí* or high king of the uilleann pipes. Séamus was born in Finglas in a house where the

would have been lost forever but for the dedication and gifts of an unparalleled musician. He believed in ghosts and in the Other World, and had a fund of stories of supernatural beings he had met in the course of his travels. He said they frequently saved his life, and there may have been some truth in his claim, for it seemed at times that only a miracle kept him going. He appeared to have more lives than the proverbial cat. He met with accidents and mishaps so numerous that they would have finished a lesser mortal, but he lived to tell the tale. Once he was found unconscious on the side of the road to Galway where he had been knocked down by a hit-and-run driver and left for dead. He recovered and went off to the Scottish Gaeltacht where he was fêted and where he gathered another bag of music.

Coming up to the end of the forties, Séamus left the Irish Folklore Commission to work for Radio Éireann. In 1954 he joined the BBC and later married an English girl. But although Séamus was a loving husband and father, he was not cut out for domesticity; as soon try to cage the golden eagle or to restrict the movements of Anthony Raftery, the blind poet of the early nineteenth century who 'was taught his music by the fairies'. In 1962 Séamus returned to the peripatetic life of playing and collecting folk music, leaving at home his five-year-old daughter Catherine, her brother Christopher and his wife Margaret. There was no bitterness. 'When we were growing up my mother was very fair about him,' Catherine once said. 'In her eyes he was still the wonderful man she married.'

Twelve years would elapse before father and daughter would meet again. 'He was still magical with children,'

Catherine remembered, 'and though I felt hurt at what I had missed out, I realised he really did sacrifice all for his music.' She inherited her father's gifts and went on to become Professor and Director of Music at St Lawrence Jewry, in the City of London. She also had the distinction of being the first female organist to hold a cathedral post at Christ Church, Oxford.

Séamus died in a caravan on the edge of what had been family land in north County Dublin. The year was 1982 and he was sixty-four. He is buried in the Naul. A celebration of his life was held some years ago when hundreds of pipers paraded round Jamestown Lodge, the old family home, and down the newly named Séamus Ennis Road. He was one of Delargy's great finds and his collection of music in the Department of Irish Folklore is testimony to his dedication to music and to the long years he cycled stony roads in search of what was all but lost.

8

GEORGIAN DUBLIN

We were bulging at the seams. In the fourteen years since the Irish Folklore Commission had been established, its base had been the three small rooms on the top corridor of University College, Earlsfort Terrace, Dublin. By now the collection of manuscripts, books, photographic material and tapes had grown to such an extent that it was impossible to find space to work. More staff were needed but there was no place to put another chair, let alone a desk or filing-cabinet. Again Michael Tierney, the President of University College, came to our rescue and on a spring day of promise in 1949 we packed everything we owned into tea-chests and transferred the lot from our eyrie in Earlsfort Terrace to 82 St Stephen's Green.

This was one of a block of buildings comprising five fine Georgian houses, Numbers 82 to 86. Number 82 was given to the Commission rent free. We had as neighbours on one side Number 83, which housed the lady Dean of Residence of the university, and on the other Iveagh House, originally the townhouse of the Guinness family. Our new home, built in the mid-eighteenth century, was four storeys high, comprising eight splendid rooms and a couple of returns as well as a large basement which served as an archive. From the flat roof, easily accessible from the top landing, it was possible to see over most of the city. The spire of St Patrick's Cathedral was one of the outstanding landmarks. From our back door we could stroll into the extensive Iveagh Gardens, on loan to the university. On summer evenings through the open windows I could hear the crack of tennis balls and the calls and laughter of students. Walks embellished with stone nymphs, shepherdesses, gods and playing fountains were a favourite rendezvous for the more romantically inclined. I had childhood memories of the Iveagh Gardens and the maypole fête where children of the poor of the city, dressed in their finery, danced round the maypoles set in a hollow and afterwards were entertained to tea and cakes.

Dublin had changed little over the centuries. It still had the elegant if slightly seedy air of an eighteenth-century buck down on his luck. A city of Georgian squares, redbrick houses, decaying mansions, slums, smoking chimneys, street traders selling everything from cockles and mussels to secondhand clothes and furniture. Men sharpened knives and scissors, sweeps offered to clean chimneys, coalmen black as the ace of spades rattled along on horsedrawn carts selling their wares by the stone, children, drawn as if by magnets, gathered around the rag-and-bone merchant offering windmills, balloons and toy monkeys on sticks in exchange for bottles and cast-off clothing.

Bird markets were held every Sunday morning in Patrick Street in the Liberties and church bells chimed out the hour. Liberty Hall, the city offices at Wood Quay, the high-rise flats of Ballymun and the British embassy on Merrion Road were nothing more than a malicious gleam in some infant architect's or town planner's eye. In the first flush of possession of our elegant house we promised ourselves that we would create a roof garden and eat our lunch alfresco whenever the sun shone. Alas there never seemed to be time.

My office was a gracious room on the ground floor and, joy of joys, I had it all to myself. It had elegantly spartan wooden floors, a handsome desk, two straight-backed chairs and a grand piano which had been presented to us by one of our staff, Janis Mezs. He was an elderly Latvian, an ex-diplomat who had sought refuge in Ireland during the war when his country was invaded by Russia. He was a gentle soul, a brilliant pianist and a fine linguist. Delargy employed him to catalogue folktales in languages other than Irish and English. Sometimes in the evening when the day's work was ended, he would come down from his room at the top of the house to play his piano, and I would sit down to enjoy a recital of classical music lasting half an hour, never longer.

At times my imagination carried me back to another age in which a carriage awaited outside the fanlit hall. I would order the coachman to take me to the Coombe where children paddled in the river Poddle that ran through Patrick Street, there greet that enigmatic clergyman, Dean Swift, as he emerged from his cathedral, chat with small dark Huguenots with high-crowned wigs as they worked their looms. Then I should drive back through the High Street and on into Grafton Street where nursemaids took the air with their aristocratic charges; and end up in the Beaux Walk on St Stephen's Green where fine ladies and fops in fancy waistcoats flirted and made assignations. The shrill cry of the telephone on my desk or some caller in need of help invariably brought me back to my own time.

According to Dublin folklore, a cross had miraculously appeared in the glass of one of the windows of Iveagh House once during Holy Week. As a schoolgirl doing the visitation of the 'seven churches' (a Holy Thursday custom said to gain a plenary indulgence for past sins) I would loiter outside the Guinness mansion, hoping to catch sight of this marvel. The story was that a Catholic maidservant in the service of the Guinness family had been denied the right to attend Mass one Holy Thursday and that ever after a cross mysteriously appeared in the window of her room. When the Guinness family generously handed over the mansion to what is now the Department of Foreign Affairs, some official decided that the cross was caused by a flaw in the glass and a new window was installed, thus putting an end to the Holy Week crowds and the legend that Dubliners loved.

When we first moved to Number 82 I was told by one of the college porters, a man who was a mine of information on old Dublin, that our offices were haunted by a beautiful lady who had had the misfortune to fall in love with a servant. Her father locked her in her bedroom where she refused all food and died soon after – some said of a broken heart. Many a time I fancied I heard the rustle of silk petticoats and saw what I took to be a ghostly figure but which on closer inspection turned out to be a shadow, a cobweb, a cupboard door.

Number 86 St Stephen's Green was named Newman House after John Henry, later Cardinal, Newman (1801-90), the great Anglican convert to Catholicism, who was first Rector of the Catholic University which had its headquarters there. By 1898, when James Joyce began his undergraduate career, it was known as University College and was part of the Royal University. Joyce spent four years there, leaving in 1902 to take up medical studies. It was during those years and within those walls that he began to formulate the creed by which he would live for the rest of his life. He revealed his thoughts to his friend and fellow student 'Cranly' (John Francis Byrne) as slightly fictionalised in *A Portrait of the Artist as a Young Man* (1916):

I will tell you what I will do and what I will not do. I will not serve that in which I no longer believe, whether it call itself my home, my fatherland, or my church: and I will try to express myself in some mode of life or art as freely as I can and as wholly as I can, using for my defence the only arms I allow myself to use - silence, exile, and cunning.

Number 86 was said to be haunted by Thomas Whaley, the eighteenth-century buck. The house was the Whaley family home and was finished in 1765. The notorious Buck Whaley had another and darker soubriquet, 'Burnchapel' Whaley. He earned this name from his habit of riding around the town on Sunday mornings tossing lighted torches on to the thatched roofs of Catholic churches, thus turning them into raging infernos and endangering the lives of the unfortunate worshippers. He was famous for a wager he made that he would reach the walls of Jerusalem and return within two years. The journey took him nine months (no mean feat in the days when the only means of transport was horseback, horse-drawn carriage or sailing ship). On his return Whaley squandered his winnings in Montpelier Lodge in the Dublin Mountains, better known as the Hellfire Club, where the rakes of the city gathered to carouse, gamble, whore and duel.

Peg Woffington, the eighteenth-century Smock Alley actress, was on one occasion abducted and taken to a black Mass in the Hellfire Club. It was said that she prayed for deliverance and the lodge went up in flames. Local people swore that they saw Satan dancing on the roof before it came crashing down. The scandal was reported in the influential *Faulkner's Dublin Journal* and the rest of the city papers took up the story. Peg was pressured to leave Ireland lest she be tempted to name names. She went to London where she became the toast of the Covent Garden and Drury Lane playhouses and the mistress of David Garrick, one of the greatest of English actors. As a child I could clearly discern the ruins of the Hellfire Club from my bedroom window, though we lived many miles away from the Dublin Mountains on the edge of the Donore Liberties.

Joyce in *A Portrait* tells of a secret staircase that was used in Whaley's time and was still in existence during his years as a university student. He has Stephen say he was 'conscious of a corruption other than that of Buck

Egan and Burnchapel Whaley'. Thankfully I never saw Whaley's ghost, but on one occasion when I went back to Number 82 rather late at night, I took the family dog with me for protection. I thought I heard a disturbance at the top of the house and, with the cheerful tailwagger accompanying me, went over all the rooms and out on to the flat roof. At first the dog gambolled and played; then, pricking up his ears as if hearing a sound beyond my ken, he gave a bloodcurdling howl and fell down in a fit, rolling his eyes in abject terror. I had to carry him back down the steps to the safety of the house, where he immediately recovered his equilibrium and set off in chase of a mouse. Newman House was in constant use as a club and restaurant for students and staff for many years. It has recently been refurbished in eighteenth-century style, is open to the public and is a must for tourists.

9

BUNRATTY CASTLE

One of the most entertaining of my colleagues during our years in 82 St Stephen's Green was Kevin Danaher. Kevin, who was born in Athea, County Limerick, in 1915, began to collect folklore while a student at UCD. He was awarded a travelling scholarship that took him to Leipzig and Berlin. He was a fund of information on pre-war Germany, telling us what went on in nightclubs and low-class dives. These, I believe, owed more to Christopher Isherwood's stories than to anything Kevin actually experienced. We were very cut off in the Ireland of the time, with censorship enforced, and so we enjoyed Kevin's exploits, albeit secondhand. He was an expert on military procedure and would demonstrate the Nazi goose-step and tell us of the hysteria that gripped the populace whenever Hitler appeared on the streets. At the outbreak of the Second World War, Kevin came back to Ireland and enlisted as a gunner in the Irish Army, rising to the rank of captain. When the war ended, he resumed his research into Irish rural life and traditions, as an ethnologist.

His service training was evident in everything he did

and said. His room was shipshape with not so much as a paperclip out of place. He was an expert mapmaker and could chart the distribution of a particular custom or tradition in exhaustive detail. He often said that his time in the army was the best of his life, though he came within a hair's breadth of death at the disaster on the Glen of Imaal practice range when soldiers to the left and right of him were blown into eternity. Like many military men, he kept his army title long after he left the service, until it was replaced by the more prestigious appellation of Doctor of Literature.

In the fifties the Commission acquired a van and Kevin took off for rural Ireland where he recorded and photographed Irish country people, their traditions and customs: fishermen, farmers and their wives, thatchers, blacksmiths, millers and travelling people. He was an authority on the craft of thatching and held that the traditional thatched roof was the glory of the Irish countryside, cool in summer and warm in winter. Thatch could be made of rushes, straw or reeds, and in rural Ireland the day of the thatching was an important event, with the neighbours gathering to help. Every schoolchild, even those who had never seen a thatched roof, let alone helped in the making of one, had been taught the old Irish proverb: '*Ní hé lá na gaoithe lá na scolb*' – 'A windy day is bad for thatching' (literally, 'The day of wind is not the day of scollops', the bent twigs that were used to fix the bundles of thatch in place).

One of the great successes of Irish tourism is Bunratty Castle and Folk Park in County Clare. The restoration of Bunratty, one of the finest surviving fifteenth-century stone fortresses in Ireland, began when it was acquired by Lord Gort in 1956. Over the years the Gorts recreated, with appropriate furniture and fittings, the atmosphere of the medieval castle where for so long the O'Briens held sway. During the centuries when Irish princes and chieftains were masters of their estates, the old traditions were observed. Food and drink flowed freely and any traveller was entitled to free and lavish hospitality. Indeed it was said that the Irish had an almost superstitious fear of turning any stranger away from their door: who knew who the stranger might be! Kuno Meyer, the noted scholar, gives this translation of an evocative passage in early Irish:

Bid thy guests welcome though they should come at every hour. Since every guest is Christ – no trifling saying this. Better is humility, better gentleness, better liberality towards him.

The Great Earl of Thomond bore the ancient title of The O'Brien, Chieftain of His Clan. No one sat in his presence except at dinner. Enthroned on his 'chair of estate', he decided quarrels, meted out justice and received rents and tithes from his tenants and followers. He was uncle to Máire Rua, the beautiful redhead we met earlier, who was born and brought up in Bunratty Castle. Today the castle and its contents are held in trust for the nation. Over the years more than a million visitors have feasted on venison, wines and mead, and been entertained with music and story at the medieval banquets held there.

From the start, Kevin Danaher was closely associated

with the restoration of Bunratty and he is largely responsible for the authenticity of the folk park, which contains a fisherman's dwelling, a weaver's shed, a blacksmith's forge and a village complete with houses, a doctor's surgery and a school – a vivid testament to how the Irish country person lived and worked a hundred or so years ago.

Kevin had an amazing memory. He claimed he could recite the whole of *Alice in Wonderland*, and often did to my exasperation when I was in the middle of a tricky piece of research or a report that demanded complete concentration. He had a fund of jokes and humorous anecdotes, equalled only by the repertoire of the late Dr Anthony Lucas, the Director of the National Museum. Once I travelled with the pair of them from Dublin to Limerick and for the entire length of the journey they capped each other's stories and jokes, while I, sick with laughter, begged them to stop. Kevin's chief attraction for the ordinary person was the collection of delightful books he wrote during the fifties and sixties dealing with Irish country people and their traditions. Possibly his best known, *The Year in Ireland* (1972), sums up his belief: 'If one were to ask what brand of folk tradition most widely reveals the Irish panorama as a whole, the answer would undoubtedly be calendar customs.'

10

'I Am Raftery the Poet'

On an autumn day in the fifties the door of 82 St Stephen's Green opened to admit a massive figure almost twenty stone in weight, whose twinkling eyes, bearded face and warm, mellow voice were familiar to people all over the world. Burl Ives, the actor and ballad singer, had arrived in Shannon and hired a car to bring him to Dublin and the offices of the Irish Folklore Commission. As in the case of Walt Disney's visit, our next door neighbours, the Department of External Affairs, had alerted us to his intended visit.

Burl Ives greeted us as though we were long-lost family, embracing us in his bear-like hug, telling us that coming to Ireland was the realisation of a cherished dream. Like almost every American I ever met, he claimed Irish blood. He had crossed the Atlantic with one idea in his mind, to follow the footsteps of Anthony Raftery, the blind poet and singer of the west of Ireland who had been born in County Mayo in 1779. Like Raftery, everyone knew of Burl Ives. He had been a professional footballer and had thrown it all up to become a vagabond, working his way across America in a variety of jobs. He was in turn labourer, sharecropper, miner and truck driver, playing his guitar and learning folk songs from hoboes and itinerant workers like himself. Together with his contemporaries Woody Guthrie and Pete Seeger, he had helped to popularise American folk music.

His travels had eventually taken him to the west coast and Hollywood, where he had gone into acting and won an Oscar for his role in the film *The Big Country*. It was for him that Tennessee Williams had written the part of Big Daddy in *Cat on a Hot Tin Roof*. His recordings of 'I Know an Old Lady' and 'Blue-Tail Fly' (a song said to have been requested by Abraham Lincoln before he gave the Gettysburg address) were played and sung in places as far apart as the black hills of Dakota and the blue hills of Antrim.

Burl Ives got down to business over a bottle of poteen he had somehow picked up along the way. His interest in Raftery, he said, had been sparked by a chance encounter in Atlanta, Georgia, with a southern gentleman whose great-great-grandmother had emigrated from County Mayo some time during the Great Famine. She had made her way south and had become housekeeper to a plantation owner who grew cotton and kept slaves. In the family folklore she was remembered as beautiful and spirited, and a very good cook. There must have been some truth to the story, for a year after her arrival she married her master and gave him a houseful of handsome sons renowned for their courage and skill in the saddle, and daughters famed for their good looks. Four were killed in the Civil War that brought the South to its knees and put an end to American slavery. The Irish mistress of the plantation never forgot her homeland and passed on to her children and grandchildren the stories and songs she had heard in the west of Ireland as a girl.

'The southern gentleman I became acquainted with had a fine baritone voice,' Burl Ives recalled, taking a swig of poteen. 'Even before I reached Atlanta I had heard of his repertoire of negro spirituals, folk songs and blues, and he didn't disappoint me. No sir, he did not! But the cream on the blueberry pie was surely the beautiful love song which he sang in the native Gaelic of his great-great-grandma. Told of a man going to church on a bright May morning and meeting this broth of a colleen called Máire Ní Eidhin at the cross of Kiltartan, who invited him back to the house for a drink. Then my friend sang another song by the same poet called "*Eanach Dhúin*", a lament for the drowning of nineteen young people in Lough Corrib when a plank in the old sailing-boat gave way.' Burl took another drink, blinked his eyes and chuckled. 'There and then I made up my mind that as soon as I had the time I would pay a visit to Ireland and find out all I could about this Anthony Raftery, maybe gather up some more of his songs.'

We were only too delighted to fill him in on blind Raftery's life and times. Indeed, any schoolchild of the time could have recited the poem that begins: '*Mise Raifterí an file, lán dóchais is grá*' ('I am Raftery the poet, full of hope and love'). Raftery's life was a mixture of tragedy, high drama and farce. Born the son of a respectable weaver, he might have been expected to follow in his father's footsteps but disaster struck in the shape

up all the folklore and music he could find and we must promise to help him with this truly worthwhile venture.

Later that evening in Kenilworth Square, Séamus Delargy got out a map and pointed out Killeenin, near Craughwell in County Galway, where Raftery was buried and where, over his grave, Lady Gregory had erected a commemorative slab sixty years before, with the help of Edward Martyn, the Catholic landlord and playwright, and Douglas Hyde. Delargy explained that it was the first two of these three who over a cup of tea on a wet Sunday afternoon in 1897 in the Comte de Bastertot's house at Duras, Kinvara in County Galway dreamed up with Yeats the idea for the various theatrical projects which would lead to the founding of the Abbey Theatre seven years later.

Burl Ives was bowled over by what he heard. He would not only gather up Raftery's songs, he would make a film of the poet and singer's life and play the part of Raftery himself. Before he embarked on this venture there was ground to cover. He would retrace Raftery's steps, hear his music, meet people who still remembered stories to do with his life. Most important of all, he would visit Raftery's grave and pay his last respects to one he called the 'greatest of the bards'. We bowed our heads in agreement and a couple of days later Ives and his entourage, together with Delargy, set off for the west of Ireland in a hired car. What followed was later recounted by Delargy whenever he was in congenial company and the name of Burl Ives cropped up. Their first port of call was Raftery's birthplace at Cill Liadáin, near Kiltimagh in County Mayo. They were told that Raftery had been abducted by the people of the *Sí* as a young boy and 'taught his music by the fairies'. There is a folktale told all over Ireland that has to do with a fiddler who had only one tune but was taken one evening by the fairies and brought to their *lios* or fairy fort. After a night of music and dancing the fiddler was left on the hillside with the fairy music still ringing in his head and tingling his fingers so that ever after he had a tune for every night of the year and became known as the best musician in Ireland. Evidently Raftery thought this story too good to waste on another musician and adapted it to suit himself, conveniently ignoring the music lessons given to him as a child by the landlord's kindly lady. This bit of fiction did him no harm. It helped to make him different from the rest of the musicians of the day, and gave him a class of distinction.

From Kiltimagh, Ives and Delargy made their way south, meeting people who remembered snippets of the folklore of Raftery's life and local historians who described the times in which he lived. Pre-Famine Ireland was a poor but merry place, an overpopulated island whose colourful, careless, unruly inhabitants loved a bit of a singsong and a dance more than anything else in the world. In the comfort of their well-sprung car the seekers after truth took stony roads over which the blind poet once tapped his way. '*Féach anois mé/Is mo chúl le balla/ Ag seinm ceóil/Do phóchaí falamh*' ('Look at me now/With my back to the wall/A-playing music/To empty pockets'), as his most famous poem puts it. John Mooney of the Department of Finance, a member of the board of the Commission, always insisted that 'with my arse (*mo thóin*) to the wall' was the correct translation.

One evening they stopped at a remote shebeen near Clarinbridge in County Galway where a group of fishermen were drinking. The men recognised Ives the moment he crossed the threshold, since they had seen *The Big Country* and knew all his ballads. Ives called for drinks on the house and in return the fishermen called for a song and were obliged with 'The Foggy Foggy Dew' and 'I Wish I Were an Apple on a Tree'. It was after midnight when, mellow with drink and hoarse with singing, they parted company with much regret and many vows of everlasting friendship. Ives said that he had enjoyed their plaudits more than all the tributes paid him when he collected his Oscar.

During the Second World War signposts all over the country had been removed by order of the government in case of enemy landings and, though a decade and more had elapsed since the war ended, many of the signs had not been restored. Mostly the travellers depended on people they met for directions but these tended to be confusing and often led them completely off the track. On this particular night they found themselves hopelessly lost. It was dark and cold and made more miserable by a mist that blotted out everything. When three cyclists minus headlamps came weaving out of a boreen, they didn't stand a chance. In a panic Ives scrambled out of the car carrying help in the shape of a bottle of whiskey, somewhat after the manner of a St Bernard dog. This was followed by coats and cushions to make the victims comfortable. Only the driver had the wit to unearth the first-aid kit. Thankfully, beyond a few scratches there was no damage done.

From where they lay on the ground, the three tipsy bachelors of uncertain age explained that they were returning from a dancehall, of the kind later made famous by William Trevor in his story 'The Ballroom of Romance', located by their pointing somewhere in the middle of the bog. Presently they were helped to their feet, brushed down and propped up against a hedge. The driver, feeling with reason that the night had gone on long enough, asked directions to Killeenin graveyard. Delargy added that they were looking for the grave of Anthony Raftery the poet. The merry trio were only too anxious to oblige with advice on the route to be taken. Sure the graveyard was no distance away at all, at all: they only had to drive up the hill, cross the bog and before long they would come to a crossroads. There was some doubt as to which road the driver should take, but sure they couldn't miss out on the graveyard where the dead of the parish had ever been buried, including this Raftery and all his seed, breed and generation. Parting, they produced a bottle of poteen out of a saddlebag, as a present to the big man from America, and not to be outdone in generosity, he gave them the bottle of whiskey, which they insisted upon sharing before making unsteady tracks for home.

It was the early hours of the morning by the time the car stopped at a graveyard overgrown with weeds. 'We've reached kingdom come,' Ives shouted, clambering over a ditch, the gate of the cemetery being locked and barred. By the light of a torch they inspected graves that had never known tombstones, others that had once borne inscriptions and were now eaten away by weather and time, still others where names were legible, but never the one they were seeking. Finally, when they had almost given up hope, they discovered a flat stone under whose green mossy weight someone called Raftery was buried. To celebrate the end of the search, they sat down on the stone, finished the poteen and waited for dawn, sobriety and enlightenment. When the sun eventually rose they discovered that they had been sitting on the grave of an old lady called Elizabeth Raftery who had died at the age of 101 a year before.

They never did find Raftery's grave, nor was the film ever made. Soon after, Burl Ives returned to California, promising to return. For years he kept in touch with us but the time never seemed to be right. There were family troubles, films he had contracted to make, ill health, promised funds that never materialised: all the obstacles that in a lifetime can come between a man and his dreams. Anthony Raftery died on Christmas Eve in 1835 and almost 160 years later, on 14 April 1995, Burl Ives followed Raftery to the grave, two months before his eighty-sixth birthday. In life they had a great deal in common: both were cult figures, both had itchy feet, both were larger than life and both shared a passion for music. Ives believed in reincarnation and told me once that in a former life he had travelled the road of Ireland, a 'dark man with a stick and the gift of poetry'. It may have been wishful thinking on his part – or indeed he may well have been Anthony Raftery as he suggested. Who can tell?

11

Away in the Bluestacks

We seldom met the full-time folklore collectors who worked mainly in Irish-speaking districts along the western seaboard: on the Dingle peninsula, around west Cork, in County Donegal and in the area of old Ulster from Rathlin Island to the Boyne. Storytelling was strongest where Irish was still the living tongue. I can safely say that without exception the collectors disliked visiting Dublin and were always anxious to get back to their bases. A collector might spend a year with a particular *seanchaí*, using as his guide the *Handbook of Irish Folklore*, which Seán O'Sullivan, the archivist of the Commission, had compiled. This was not only a book of questions but also an encyclopaedia of traditions, a treasure house of fact and fancy, ritual and observance, custom and belief. If it had never been written, it is unlikely that the great body of Irish folklore amounting to almost two thousand large bound volumes and collected between 1935 and 1971 would ever have been amassed. In addition, the Irish Folklore Commission brought with it to University College, Belfield, in 1971 a music collection of manuscripts, tapes and recordings, a specialised library of 25,000 books, periodicals and papers, as well as a photographic collection and a gallery of original paintings and drawings.

Over the years I got to know the collectors well. They were, in the main, quiet, bookish men who had trained as teachers, had an abiding interest in folklore and had been persuaded by Delargy to abandon the careers they were following to become workers in the field. From time to time I would visit parts of the country where they worked and sometimes they could be coaxed into introducing me to their informants and showing me places of interest. Over the years the Irish Folklore Commission employed twenty full-time folklore collectors, some of whom became friends of mine.

My earliest recollection is of meeting Tadhg Ó Murchú and his wife Máire. Tadhg lived in Waterville, County Kerry, and we saw more of him than the rest of the collectors put together. This was largely because Máire loved coming to Dublin. They always stayed in the Swiss Chalet in Merrion Row, in those days a pâtisserie that sold delicious cakes and bread and kept a small number of privileged guests. To the Ó Murchús it was 'home from home'.

Máire and Tadhg were in their forties when I got to know them well. Tall and handsome, they had the blond hair and blue eyes of their Norman ancestors (both had FitzGerald blood in their veins) and a zest for life that promised a rich old age. While he said little, she hardly ever drew breath. As is the way with many couples who have no children, they mothered each other. She invariably addressed him as 'Tadhg, *a chroí*' and, while he was a man of few words, the delight she gave him showed in his eyes. He could deny her nothing and when she was in Dublin I spent all my spare time shopping with her in Grafton Street or going to the pictures, which she particularly loved.

We would eat supper in the Unicorn Restaurant across the way from the Swiss Chalet and she would boast of her friends in the Butler Arms Hotel, a stone's throw from their home. She was friendly with Charlie Chaplin and his wife Oonagh who came to stay for a month each year in the Waterville Arms Hotel. Oonagh gave Máire a small birthstone ring which she took with her to the grave.

I had the only occult experience of my life while working with Tadhg. I was staying in a modest hotel in nearby Kenmare. It was a marvellous summer, the kind we get in Ireland about once in a decade: brilliantly sunny days and balmy nights. Yet I was chilled to the marrow each time I put my foot inside my hotel bedroom. Bedtime was a nightmare. Later, back in Dublin, I discovered that a young clerical student had taken his life in the room that I had occupied and where I experienced so deep a depression that it still chills me.

I never told Tadhg or Máire of my experience. Tadhg did not believe in ghosts any more than the rest of the collectors, while Máire would have been so upset she would have have insisted on my staying with them and she often had a house full of guests. She said that if anything happened to Tadhg she would not live long after him. This I found hard to believe. Then one day she phoned to tell me that she had heard the banshee. She thought the messenger of death had come for her. Soon after, Tadhg died of a heart attack and within twelve months Máire had followed him to the grave. I never heard what illness she had, if any. I believe she died of a broken heart.

When Delargy recruited Michael J. Murphy (1913–96) first as part-time and later as full-time folklore collector, or 'cultural intelligence officer', as Michael liked to put it, he was already popular as a broadcaster for the BBC in Belfast and had written books on the folklore of the northeast. Between 1949 and 1983 he covered most of the northeast, spending long periods on Rathlin Islands, in the Antrim Glens, the Mournes, Fermanagh, Tyrone and Armagh. His informants were of every class and creed, Protestant, Catholic and Dissenter, and were proud to have the folklore of their ancestors recorded. He helped us film and record the traditional Orange processions at the Field at Finaghy in the days before darkness descended on the six counties of the northeast. He wrote more than a dozen plays and books dealing with the Irish countryside and gathered what is probably the largest collection of oral tradition anywhere in the English-speaking world.

Benedict Kiely, who was a constant visitor to the Commission, first met Michael in 1950 and said of him:

This man beside me is a druid from the land round Finn MacCool's mountain in South Armagh. He is as much a part of this ancient land as the stone he sits on. He could have been here on this hillside under this oak before St Patrick came.

I mourned the death of a good friend when Michael died on 17 May 1996.

Of all the collectors, probably the best known was Seán Ó hEochaidh, whose wife Anna was postmistress of Gortahork and who for more than forty years collected the folklore of his native Donegal, making odd sorties into the neighbouring county of Derry. Donegal was for centuries a place apart and its people were renowned for their hospitality. Long after the downfall of the aristocratic Gaelic civilisation in the rest of Ireland, the old way of life lingered on there. Ó hEochaidh started life as a fisherman. He owned a boat and would undoubtedly have ended up with a fishing fleet and made a fortune, but neither money nor fame interested him. I was delighted when years later he was honoured by the university with the title of Doctor of Literature. He had a dedication to the work he was doing and a vast admiration for the storytellers with whom he spent his life. He was also an expert on the lore and tradition of the sea.

Donegal, like Derry, lays legitimate claim to St Columcille. He was born in Gartan, about seven miles from Letterkenny, in 521, less than a century after Patrick had lit the paschal fire at Tara. They had been golden years for Ireland and had changed the temper of the old bloody pagan days. Columcille could have ruled Ireland; he came of kingly stock. Instead he became a cleric. A well known unhistorical story has it that the saint fell seriously in love, not with a beautiful maiden but with his spiritual master's psalter, uniquely decorated, highly cherished and not for sale. When he couldn't come by it legally, Columcille is said to have decided to acquire it by stealth, and made a copy of the psalter, to which, naturally enough, Finian, its owner, objected. Columcille was summoned before Diarmait, the high king, to answer the charge of theft and was ordered to return the copy he had made. The king's traditional judgement was: 'To every cow belongs its calf and to every book its little copy.' It was Ireland's first copyright case.

Columcille is remembered as a handsome man, albeit rather bandy. Ó hEochaidh collected many legends that illustrated not only the saint's style and personal pride but also his sharp and ready tongue. Once, so the story goes, when out fishing, Columcille encountered a shoal of flounders. 'Is this a removal?' the saint enquired jocosely. 'Yes it is, crooked-legs,' a pert young flounder shot back, falling about laughing. Columcille was not amused: 'If I have crooked legs, may you have a crooked mouth,' he retorted. And to this day if you care to look you will see that the flounder has a crooked mouth.

Many visiting scholars and writers found their way to Ó hEochaidh's home and when the time came for them to leave, they had learned much about the folklore, archaeology and history of Donegal and had gained some fluency in the Irish language, thanks to Seán's enthusiasm and teaching gifts.

He was particularly devoted to his father-in-law, Michael Mac Gabhann, who lived at Cashel near Gortahork. Over the gateway of the house was the skeleton of a sea serpent that had been washed up on Magheraroarty strand. Local folklore had it that the serpent, in trying to swallow a fishing boat, had choked to death. Mickey, as he was known far and wide, had emigrated as a young man to Scotland and then made his way to America where he worked in the steel mills of Pennsylvania. He returned to Ireland in 1901 and bought the 'house of the serpent', so dubbed by the locals, for the sum of one thousand pounds, at that time a sizable amount of money. He had brought back with him a small fortune, having successfully panned for pay-dirt in the Klondike gold rush of the late 1890s.

Mickey dictated his adventures to Ó hEochaidh, and the young folklore collector courted and married his daughter Anna. The autobiography was published as *Rotha Mór an tSaoil* in 1959 and translated into English three years later by Valentin Iremonger as *The Hard Road to the Klondike*. When I first visited Gortahork, Seán kept me enthralled one winter's night by the turf fire with stories of Mickey's adventures. I can still remember the background noise of the waves crashing upon the rocks outside and Seán's lilting Donegal accent recounting how one St Patrick's Day when Mickey was mining a seam, from over a hill came the sound of music, and a lone piper playing a poignant Irish air marched into view. At once Mickey and his companions – Irishmen all – forgot about gold, downed tools and, like the children of Hamelin, followed the piper to the next town, where they spent the rest of the day and a good part of the night celebrating Ireland's national feast in the time-honoured manner. Mickey said it was the most enjoyable St Patrick's Day he had ever spent.

Mickey died on 29 November 1948 in his eighty-third year. A decade later, when *Rotha Mór an tSaoil* was published, Seán presented me with a copy of Mickey's story. On the flyleaf he had written the old man's epitaph: 'The pen's trace remains though the hand that held it dies.'

On one occasion Seán took me to visit a famous storyteller, Anna Nic a' Luain. We left Gortahork on the last day of the old year and drove south to a remote glen at the foot of the Bluestacks, about thirty miles away, where sheep outnumbered humans by thousands, and where Anna lived alone. I can still see her, a handsome woman in her late sixties, with high cheekbones, lustrous dark hair and lively eyes. She had used the wool of her own sheep to spin, dye and knit.

Anna loved plants and wild flowers. She was expert in the making of traditional dyes and was also known locally as a herbalist and folk doctor. This was often the case with such people – not surprisingly, seeing that a good knowledge of plants and herbs is necessary for both skills. She showed me autumn crocus (*crocus sativus*), in Irish *cróch an fhómhair*, which gave the yellow dye she had used for her wool, and which is in addition a cure for measles. Then there was foxglove (*digitalis purpurea*) which is known in Irish as *méaracáin na mban sí* (banshee thimbles) and produces a green dye. Digitalis was once widely used for heart disease. Outside Anna's door grew wild pansy (*viola lutea*), in Irish *goirmín sléibhe*, which dyed blue and was a remedy for constipation, while pennywort (*umbilicus ruprestis*), known as *carnán caisil* or *lus na pingine*, was used as a yellow dye and was also a popular folk cure for a variety of ailments from chilblains to tuberculosis. Ivy removed warts, while nettles made into a brew relieved rheumatism, sciatica and pleurisy; this was popular as a spring tonic for the blood.

Purple, the colour of kings, could be obtained from certain shellfish found round the coast. A plant called Our Lady's Bedstraw (*galium verum*), in Irish *rú Mhuire*, got its name from the belief that it was one of the herbs in Christ's manger at Bethlehem. It is one of the few native plants to yield a red dye and at one time it was used for curdling milk to make cheese.

Anna had never gone further afield than the town of Donegal and had lived all her sixty-seven years in her one-room thatched cottage, which contained a settle bed, a well-scrubbed table, a bench, a *súgán* chair and a dresser of delph. From the chimney it was possible to see the sky. Anna had been expecting our arrival and had cooked a delicious mutton broth flavoured with wild garlic and herbs in a pot-oven on the open hearth. A gipsy had taught her how to tell fortunes and after the meal of mutton, followed by tea and soda bread, she read my future in the tea-leaves. She told me I would be unlucky in love and blessed in friendship, and that one day I would write this book. Afterwards Seán told me she was gifted with second sight.

She had much lore about death customs and beliefs: the shadow of a black coffin on the surface of a nearby lake foretold a drowning. A spectral funeral seen at midnight spelt disaster, while hares behaving strangely, a footprint found in the ashes of the fire on Easter Sunday morning or strange lights in empty houses were all taken as warnings of imminent death.

Seán, like the rest of the collectors, had little belief in superstitions or charms, but under duress he told me how as a lad he had seen his favourite uncle walk along the passage that ran through his home, while in fact the man was cutting hay on his farm miles away. Call it co-incidence or what you will, but as the figure made its ghostly way out the door, the uncle dropped in his tracks and was dead before help could be summoned. Such a spirit – an apparition of a living person seen somewhere else before death – is known in Irish and other folklores as a 'fetch'.

As I bade farewell to Anna that New Year's Eve, she wrapped a griddle cake which had been cooling on the windowsill in newspaper and pressed it into my hands. She said travellers should always carry bread in their pockets lest they should stumble on 'hungry grass' and die of starvation. It was customary to use crusts of bread instead of coins to close the eyes of a dead gipsy or traveller. I stood with Seán at the door of the cottage under a sky full of stars while we made our farewells. Away in the distance the Bluestacks rose stark and desolate. In cottage windows dotting the mountainside candles flickered, lit in honour of the birth of the new year. I never saw Anna again, but I never forgot with what dignity she made her offering. It was all she had. It was the best gift I ever received.

Professor Séamus Delargy, Director of the Irish Folklore Commission (1965)

Some of the founder members of the Irish Folklore Commission (1937): left to right: Seán Mac Giollarnáth; Séamus Delargy, Director; an tAthair Eric Mac Fhinn; Adolph Mahr; Professor Osborne J. Bergin; Peadar Mac Fhionnlaoich; Liam Praigheas; Reverend John G. O'Neill; Leon Ó Broin; Éamonn Ó Donnchadha; Louis Maguire; Professor Åke Campbell

Tadhg Ó Murchú and his wife Máire, an Coireán, Waterville, County Kerry (1956)

Kevin Danaher in Kerry (1946)

Séamus Ennis taking notes from Colm Ó Caodháin in Carna,
County Galway (1947)

Máire MacNeill, working in the archives of the Irish Folklore
Commission (1947)

Donegal folklore collector Seán Ó hEochaidh (left) with Ciarán Ó Síocháin (*c.* 1960)

Michael J. Murphy, whom Benedict Kiely described as 'a druid from the land round Finn MacCool's mountain in South Armagh' (1950)

Peig Sayers (1946)

Anna Nic a'Luain, na Cruacha, County Donegal (1949)

Seosamh Ó Dálaigh recording from Cáit Ruiséal, Baile Ic Fhinn, County Kerry (c. 1942)

Seán Ó Sullivan, archivist (1903–96) (1996)

Nils Holmer taking down a story from M. Hynes, Bishop's Quarter, County Clare (1949)

Bríd Mahon (1968)

12

—

St Brigid's Cloak

We gathered what information we could on patterns, wakes, weddings, harvest festivals and the four quarters of the year – St Brigid's Eve, May Eve, Midsummer Eve and November Eve – when bonfires were lit on the mountains and magic was all around. The year in Ireland was traditionally held to commence on 1 February, St Brigid's Day. Many believe that in the persona of Brigid we find both the Christian saint and the pagan goddess once widely worshipped. All over Ireland many customs and beliefs were associated with her feast. Butter was always freshly churned on St Brigid's Day and a cake as big as a cartwheel made of flour, curds, milk and eggs. A length of cloth or ribbon, known as *Brat Bhríde,* was left outside the door on the eve of the feast for Brigid to bless as she passed by with her pet cow. The *brat* was used as a cure for headache and toothache. Brigid's crosses woven from plaited rushes or straw were hung from the ceiling and lintel of the dwelling-house, and around the dairy, to ensure health and prosperity for the coming year. I was sorry when RTÉ dropped the traditional St Brigid's cross

as its logo. For fifteen hundred years it had been a part
of the Irish way of life.

Both in the written sources and in folklore St Brigid
comes across as charismatic, warm-hearted and hospitable, as liberated as any woman who ever drew breath.
In her day she wielded immense authority, travelled
widely, entertained with grace and gave freely to the poor
and needy. She was reputed to be the best maker of ale
and mead in Ireland and to have enjoyed her drink as well
as the next.

Everyone knows the story of how she outwitted a
mendacious king, who promised her as much land as
could be covered by her cloak. One version says that the
cloak miraculously stretched to cover the land she
needed, but another and more likely account tells how she
cut up the cloth into tiny strips, which she placed in a
circle wide enough to encompass the whole of the Curragh
of Kildare. She kept the king to his word and built a
monastery. This was in time to become the principal
foundation of the kingdom of Leinster, one part being for
monks under the jurisdiction of an abbot-bishop, the
other being reserved for nuns. It is said that the Abbess
Brigid in fact ruled the entire foundation, keeping the
bishop only for purposes of ordination.

In the year 650, 124 years after Brigid's death, a cleric
known as Cogitosus wrote one of many biographies. In it
he included a charming legend. It seems that the king of
Leinster had a pet fox of which he was immensely proud.
By mistake a shepherd killed the fox and in a fury the
king sentenced him to death. Relenting a little, the king
said that his life would be spared if he could produce a

fox the equal in skill and intelligence of his lost pet. That evening a wild fox came to Brigid's monastery and in the space of a night she taught the animal so well that it not only equalled but outpaced the dead pet in accomplishment and sagacity. The fox was duly presented at court the next day and the king was so delighted he promptly pardoned the shepherd. Shortly after, the shepherd left Leinster to seek work in another kingdom. The moment the shepherd took his departure, the fox escaped from the court, to return to the waters and the wild.

In 1984 I set out for Bruges in the hope of recovering St Brigid's cloak, which had been presented to the Flemish people by the Saxon princess Gunhild almost a thousand years before. The story goes that Gunhild's brother Harold, on a visit from Britain to Dermot of Leinster, attended the shrine of the saint in Kildare. He took away some relics, including her legendary cloak, in the hope that they would help him defeat the Normans who were threatening his Saxon kingdom. Miracles seldom happen in that way and Harold lost the Battle of Hastings in 1066 to William the Conqueror. Saxon rule was virtually finished, the Normans were there to stay and Gunhild fled England for the Lowlands bringing the legendary cloak in her baggage.

Up to the Second World War the effigy of St Brigid was paraded through the streets of Bruges each year on her feast. Now, alas, she is forgotten and the venerable cloak, once revered by the Belgian people, is relegated to the back of a dusty ecclesiastical museum in the cathedral of St Salvator in Bruges. I made Trojan efforts to have the cloak returned where it belongs, to Kildare cathedral. I even wrote to the late Cardinal Tomás Ó Fiaich for help. He was sympathetic and did what he could but the Belgian hierarchy refused to budge.

It is a pity that the custom of lighting hill bonfires in the four quarters of the year has died out. It must have been quite a spectacle to see a chain of light stretching across Ireland. These were the nights when magic was at its most potent, when the people of the *Sí* changed residence, when potions and spells were used, music and dancing were enjoyed and the storyteller came into his own.

St John's Eve, 23 June, was traditionally Midsummer Day. Herbs gathered at this time of year were said to be especially powerful. St John's Wort (*hypericum*), in Irish *luibh Eoin Bhaiste*, was known as the fairy herb because of its curative properties. When crushed, it gave off the odour of incense and was said to be a protection and have special powers against the evils of witchcraft. It was used for the treatment of rheumatism and bruises, and a remedy for the 'airy fit' (an attack of depression).

Hallowe'en, the vigil of the ancient festival of Samhain, is still enjoyed by children playing 'trick or treat' while dressed up as witches, goblins and ghosts. In the early days of the Commission our leave was limited to eighteen days a year but we always celebrated the feast of Samhain, 1 November, by an extra day's holiday. On Hallowe'en we would work late. A custom of exchanging small gifts had grown up, after which we would make a meal of sorts. I can still see the kettle boiling on the turf fire in our old rooms in Earlsfort Terrace. Seán O'Sullivan, who was senior, made very strong tea and the rest of us contributed apples, nuts, barmbrack and for some reason a dish of fudge.

This was the night when with any luck you could find out what the future would hold. If you slept on a sprig of yarrow, you would dream of a lover. You might also put two nuts named for yourself and your loved one together on the hob in the hope that they would jump off together – a good augury for the future. There was a charm in peeling an apple to see if the skin formed the initial of your partner and, to find out his assets, it was best to pluck up a head of cabbage. The size and shape of the roots denoted the type he would be: straight and sturdy or withered and crabbed; rich and generous if a decent lump of clay adhered to the roots, poor and mean if there was little or nothing there. On one occasion, having exhausted all the spells we knew, Kevin Danaher combed the works of Brian Merriman, the eighteenth-century Clare schoolmaster and author of the great satirical poem *Cúirt an Mheán-Oíche* (1780), to see what he had to say. He came up with:

> *Under my pillow, I've kept all night*
> *A stocking stuffed with apples tight*
> *For hours a pious fast kept up*
> *Without a thought of bite or sup*
> *My shift I've drawn against the stream*
> *In the hopes of my future love to dream.*

I have the feeling that Brian Merriman might not have been too pleased at the attempt at translation of his verse but truth is stranger than fiction and that night I met a

102

man I might have married, if fate had not intervened, and Kevin found the dark and pretty Limerick girl he was to wed before twelve months had elapsed.

In pre-Christian Ireland the winter solstice, which occurs on 21 December, was the time of the year when the dead were said to return. I felt the strength of this 7,000-year-old belief inside Newgrange, one of the three great burial mounds in the Boyne valley (the others being Knowth and Dowth). These burial sites are older than Stonehenge and much older than the Pyramids of Egypt. We know nothing of the race of people who built the tombs, save that they were artists, skilled builders and had an amazing knowledge of astronomy.

One year I waited inside Newgrange with a group of archaeologists who had travelled from distant parts in the hope that the ancient magic would take place. And it did. As dawn broke we saw the light of the rising sun push its way through the fanlight above the main entrance. Slowly, bewitchingly, like a golden stream, it travelled down the narrow passage, finally to flood with aureate light the magnificent chamber where we waited. It was an awe-inspiring sight: clearly visible all around were intricately carved stones and cremation basins which aeons ago held the ashes of dead kings, queens and princes. We marvelled at the genius of the ancient builders who left behind their testimony of a spirit world and their belief that the dead returned.

Of all the festivals of the year Christmas was, and still is, considered the most important in Ireland. People continue to decorate their homes with holly and ivy, and light the Christmas candle. It was once a common belief that the gates of heaven were opened during the twelve days of Christmas and that anyone who died then went straight to paradise. Pious people, as well as those who wished to enjoy good health and longevity, fasted and abstained from meat on Christmas Eve and again on Boxing Day in honour of St Stephen, the first martyr, whose day it was. And not a bad idea at that after a surfeit of feasting.

Little Christmas or *Nollaig na mBan* (women's Christmas), which fell on 6 January, ended the festive season. This day also celebrated the coming of the Three Wise Men who followed their star from the east until they reached the city of David and found the child. They are most joyously remembered in the Irish tradition, as is the belief that in their honour, on this their night, the waters of the world are turned to wine.

13

THE HOBBIT

I had always wanted to meet the author of *The Hobbit* (1937), which as most of you know is a book about Bilbo Baggins, a character about the size of an Irish leprechaun. Bilbo lived in a well set-up and comfortable hole in the ground. Had he lived today his home would have had a fridge-freezer, microwave, television, video recorder, telephone and E-mail receptor. The walls would have been fashionably panelled in wood, the floors carpeted, the picture-windows overlooking a landscaped garden with possibly a river running along at the end – a bit difficult I'll admit in even the best holes in the ground. In other words, the kind of highly desirable residence for which you would need either to win the lottery or discover a crock of gold.

As well as their height, hobbits had other traits in common with leprechauns: round fat stomachs and brightly coloured clothes. They refused to grow beards, unlike the fairy shoemakers, but they too possessed long brown clever fingers, good-natured faces and deep belly laughs. These simple little English creatures had no time for charms and spells and would indulge only in the ordinary everyday kind of magic that enabled them to vanish silently when large, stupid folk like you and me came blundering along.

While still at school I had read and re-read Bilbo's epic adventures when he was forced to journey from his cosy home in Hobbiton through the perilous Misty Mountains to do battle with trolls, goblins and dragons. Now, twenty years on, I was about to meet Bilbo's creator – or should I say biographer? – Professor J. R. R. Tolkien. *The Hobbit* and *The Lord of the Rings* (1954–55) had been translated into twenty-four languages and had sold millions of copies. Professor Tolkien was arriving to meet a former student of his, Thomas P. Dunning, a Vincentian Father and Professor of Middle English at UCD. He was anxious to learn something of Irish folklore, and Father Dunning, an old friend, had promised to introduce him to the Irish Folklore Commission.

Tolkien was a man in his early sixties when we met, with a mane of white hair which he wore brushed back from a high forehead, a Roman nose and laughter lines. I asked him if he had modelled Bilbo Baggins on Mr Badger from Kenneth Grahame's *The Wind in the Willows* (1908), who also lived in a well-furnished and comfortable hole in the ground; or possibly he had Mr Toad of Toad Hall in mind. Without batting an eyelid, he told me that he had come across Bilbo Baggins's memoirs by chance in a densely written and obscure manuscript in the Bodleian Library in Oxford. 'The chronicle of course had to be modernised and turned into English as far as possible,' he explained gravely. 'In some ways it was not too difficult. In Bilbo's time the speech was a sort of lingua franca, made up of all sorts of languages and known as the Common Speech. If hobbits ever had any special language of their own they had long since given it up for they were not great linguists.' I was always sorry that I did not get Tolkien to give me this explanation in writing. I later heard that he had written a letter to two young girls in Scotland during the Second World War. One would not wish to sell such a unique document; still and all, that letter fetched thousands of pounds when auctioned at Sotheby's a couple of years ago.

Professor Tolkien had a wide knowledge of Irish writing and writers. He particularly admired the work of Sean O'Faolain and was anxious to meet him. In the euphoria of our meeting I said I would arrange a little supper party at which the two could exchange views. It was not that I knew Sean O'Faolain at all well – we were barely acquainted – but his wife Eileen, a charming woman, often dropped into the Commission and I had given her some help when she was doing research in our archives for a book of Irish folktales which she later had published.

Among a variety of subjects, Tolkien was interested in regional foods. Yet he could by no means be described as a gourmet. He was a man of simple tastes but he liked to know why certain peoples ate certain dishes at certain times of the year. I had been researching traditional food and drink, and when I have information to impart, I am inclined to overwhelm my listeners with facts and figures. Tolkien enquired politely about Irish soda bread, which I dismissed as a nineteenth-century latecomer, instead

waxing enthusiastic about Irish whiskey, which is mentioned in the *Annals of the Four Masters* under the year
1405. Later on it was a favourite tipple of Elizabeth I. Next
I spoke earnestly of honey, which played so important a
part in the diet of early Ireland that a special section of
the Brehon Laws was devoted to bees and beekeeping.
And as for Irish salmon, it has always been the favourite
food, not only of kings and heroes, but also of hermits
and anchorites, who might permit themselves a portion
garnished with watercress. I told the story of how Finn
MacCool got the first taste of the salmon of knowledge
and became the wisest man in Ireland. Thereafter, in his
wisdom, he baked the fish with sorrel leaves. Tolkien
smacked his lips and said that sounded delicious.

Would that I had stopped at that. There is nothing to
baked salmon with sorrel sauce. I could cook it blindfold.
But no! I was well into my stride, touching on the twelfth-
century *Aislinge meic Conglinne* (*The Vision of Mac
Conglinne*) which is undoubtedly the finest single record
of food eaten in medieval Ireland and in which corned
beef gets favourable mention. I declared that the Irish
relished corned beef above all meats when cooked with
cabbage and floury potatoes, and that millions who fled
to America during and after the Great Famine carried with
them the memory of this festive dish. 'A tradition that
survives in America to this very day,' I said conclusively.
'If you happen to visit America and mention that you are
Irish, that is just what you will get.'

Tolkien, with a twinkle in his eye, said he must sample
this important food before he left Ireland and in a
moment of insanity I said I would cook it for him for the

supper party I had promised. The night should have been a success. I laid on a plentiful supply of Guinness, which Tolkien said he would prefer to wine with the robust dish we were going to eat. The company too bade fair to be entertaining. Together with Sean and Eileen O'Faolain I had invited Tom Dunning, who was an excellent raconteur and an old friend, Alice Martin, secretary to Fine Gael, with all the political gossip at her fingertips, and, of course, the guest of honour, J. R. R. Tolkien himself.

Sean arrived late and minus Eileen who was down with flu. That meant rearranging the table at the last moment. Things went from bad to worse. The trouble may have been that the turf was damp and refused to light, that the corned beef was undoubtedly tough, that the smell of cabbage permeated the house or that the potatoes were overcooked. Or that Sean was going down with flu like his wife. Whatever the reason, bite nor sup never passed his lips and he scarcely opened his mouth for the length of the night. The rest of us made strenuous efforts to pull the party together but it was as if a pall of gloom had settled on the table. At ten o'clock my guests rose to their feet and beat a hasty retreat to the door. I could hear their merry cries of relief as they walked down the street.

My final meeting with Tolkien was when Delargy invited us to his usual Saturday night gathering in Kenilworth Square. That night the talk was lively, a fire of turf and wood gave out a good heat and a wholesome smell, Tolkien had brought whiskey and Delargy provided sherry and the usual tea and toasted scones. It was almost midnight by the time we left, Tolkien, Dunning and I sharing a taxi. Halfway down Rathmines Road, Tolkien spied a chip shop and said he rather fancied something to eat. We dismissed the taxi and Tolkien ordered three large helpings of fish and chips which he insisted be wrapped in newspaper, declaring that the printer's ink gave the food a distinctive flavour.

The remainder of the night is imprinted on my memory – a time set apart, when we were one in spirit, and ideas came like bolts of lightning. We found ourselves strolling along the banks of the Grand Canal, happily eating mouthwatering ray and golden chips, well baptised with vinegar, using our fingers as forks. We finished up at an all-night 'greasy spoon' in Baggot Street drinking excellent coffee into which we dunked our doughnuts, while we discussed the survival of ancient pilgrimages. I told Tolkien how up to quite recently it was the custom in many parts of the country to visit holy wells on the feast of a local saint and drink the waters in the hope of a cure. In return Tolkien gave me Canterbury, the famous English medieval pilgrimage, and described the Wife of Bath, with five husbands behind her and on the lookout for a sixth. He seemed to have Chaucer's masterpiece by heart, quoting snippets of *The Canterbury Tales* with such feeling that we might have been back in the fourteenth century travelling the pilgrims' way with the poet himself. What especially gladdened my heart was to discover that Tolkien also knew all 110 of the *Kinder- und Hausmärchen (Children's and Household Tales)* of the Brothers Grimm. The Grimms had been collectors of folklore from at least 1800 and we had versions of their tales in our archives, for they are internationally known. These stories were the first my parents read me, and that early start gave me a great advantage when I took up my first (and only) job, folklorist with the Commission.

I was never to meet Professor Tolkien again. He died in 1973 at the age of eighty-one, having had many honours bestowed on him. I can't be sure, however, that his ghost isn't somewhere out there, chuckling at my reminiscences and the memory of that disastrous supper party when I dished up food fit only for Smaug, the large and very fierce dragon whom Bilbo Baggins encountered so long ago on his dangerous quest.

14

DUBLIN FOLKLORE

I hold the name of Séamus Delargy, first Professor of Irish Folklore at UCD and Honorary Director of the Irish Folklore Commission, in the greatest esteem. He was a remarkable and far-seeing man, an inspired teacher and prose writer, and he had the gift of imbuing others with his passion and dedication. If he drove us hard, he did not spare himself. When I first met him he had a shock of red hair and a temper, which he did his best to subdue, to match. He was a dedicated angler and, to our relief, the moment he heard the mayfly was up each year he took off for Altnabrocky Lodge in County Mayo. There for a couple of weeks he would forget his woes. These were mainly caused by worries about the work of collection and the need to meet targets with the slender grant-in-aid the Department of Education allowed us. Post-war Ireland was changing rapidly, and, as he never tired of telling us, our work was a fight against time. He was also genuinely concerned that Irish religious and educationalists in the mission fields, taking their cue from the colonists, ignored the culture and traditions of the native population they were dealing with. He had even approached the Vatican but to no avail. He warned that, when independence came to those countries, their leaders would not easily forget this shameful neglect – and he was to be proved right.

Besides fishing, Séamus Delargy enjoyed reading detective stories. Georges Simenon, the Belgian creator of the French detective Maigret, was his favourite author. He was no film buff but enjoyed the antics of Laurel and Hardy. He once told me that when threatened with depression, a condition that overtook him frequently, he only had to sit back in his seat, close his eyes, conjure up pictures in his mind's eye of the two great comedians and God was in his heaven again and all right with the world. One thing I shall always regret is his lack of interest in urban traditions, and more especially in those of Dublin. Our main task lay in gathering up the folk tradition of Gaelic Ireland before it was too late. Everything else must take second place. Unfortunately, in those years I was the only woman folklorist and the only Dubliner on the staff.

Both my parents were city born. By the time I was ten years old I had imbibed much of the culture and traditions of old Dublin. In my mother's youth, funeral games which were pagan in origin were still being played at wakes in the Liberties. 'The Priest of the Parish has Lost his Considering Cap' was a runaway favourite, with its daring forfeits and sexual overtones. The players stood in a circle and the cap was passed round behind backs. Whoever was found with the cap had to pay a forfeit, kissing all the members of the opposite sex or going outside with 'the one you loved best' for a 'court'.

At the other end of the spectrum were the Dublin street games I had played as a child: hopscotch and 'beds', 'Ghost in the Garden', which was guaranteed to send a highly strung child shrieking for home and safety. The best games were those that were playlets in themselves, requiring a 'lead' and a cast of extras. I remember sunny days when we split into two groups, one group forming an arch under which the second would parade to the chant: 'Here come the robbers passing by, passing by.' There was the game that began, 'The great big ship sailed through the Alley-O' (which was based, it was said, on the disaster of the *Titanic*). 'Ring a Roses', when we sneezed and all fell down, recalled, they say, the Great Plague of 1665–66 in London. Perhaps the most colourful and dramatic game, and my favourite, was:

Stands a lady on the mountains.
Who she is I do not know.
All she wants is gold and silver
And a nice young man to love her.

This game required at least a dozen players and included a prologue, a search, a love scene and a wedding. The newlyweds would go down from the mountains to the city and call out, 'Open the gates and let me through', while the rest of us citizens called back, 'Not till you show your black and blue.' Researching the life and times of Peg Woffington some years ago, I came upon an eighteenth-century account of the game, with the youthful Peg playing the part of the 'lady on the mountains'.

The Liberties had a rich seam of old Dublin folklore.

As a youngster on my way to school I used to stand with my nose pressed to the window of a huckster's shop in Faddle Alley, Black Pitts, where treacle toffee guaranteed to wreak havoc with the strongest teeth was displayed. It was in this house that Michael Moran (1794-1846), ballad singer and Dublin's last gleeman, was born. Like his rural counterpart, Anthony Raftery, Moran went blind as a child and thereafter used his wits and his talent at versemaking to eke out a living. He could be described as the original Dublin 'busker'. W. B. Yeats tells us in his book of essays *The Celtic Twilight* (1893) how Moran got the inspiration for his verse:

In the morning when he had finished his breakfast his wife or some neighbour would read the news-papers out to him, and read on and on until he interrupted with 'That'll do. I have me meditations.'

From these meditations would come the day's story of jest and rhyme. He had the whole of the Middle Ages under his coat. His poem 'St Mary of Egypt' relates how a certain Bishop Zozimus converted a lady of easy virtue who lived in Egypt. Soon after, she died in the odour of sanctity. 'St Mary of Egypt' became so popular and was so often repeated that Moran earned the appellation 'Zozimus'. He composed a poem called 'Moses' and it is by this that he is best remembered today. During the forties an old beggarman whose pitch was the corner of Francis Street and Cornmarket used to earn a crust by reciting the poem:

On Egypt's banks, contagious to the Nile,
King Pharaoh's daughter, went to bathe in style.
She tuk her dip, then walked unto the land,
To dry her royal pelt she ran along the strand.
A bullrush tripped her, whereupon she saw,
A smiling babby in a wad o' straw;
She tuk it up and said with accents mild,
'Tar-and-agers, girls, now, which av yez owns the
child?'

Michael Moran, alias Zozimus, died at the age of fifty-two in a tenement house in Patrick Street in 1846, surrounded by a roomful of balladeers and fiddlers come to cheer his end and to accompany him on his last journey. Unhappily the hearse was overweight and before the cortège had left the street the spring collapsed. Whereupon one of the musicians produced a bottle of whiskey and the mourners sat down on the cobbles to drink to the dead. Some say that Zozimus sat up in his coffin demanding his share and gave a spirited rendition of the ballad with which he had been in the habit of starting his day:

Gather round me, boys, will yez
And hear what I have to say
Before old Sally [his wife] brings me
Me bread and jug o'tay.

Belief in ghosts has waned, though sightings of flying saucers and other UFOs are on the increase. Ghostly manifestations are nowadays put down to traumatic experiences which have somehow imprinted themselves on the stratosphere and are picked up by receptive persons. In the Ireland of the past, ghosts were commonplace; many houses were haunted and certain uneasy spirits knew no rest. Dublin was no different from the rest of the country in this respect, and perhaps its most gruesome ghost was that of a man who not only abused his children but drove his wife to an early grave. In a drunken fit he fell down the stairs of the tenement house where he lived in Francis Street and broke his neck. Almost immediately his ghost began haunting not only the street but the lanes and alleyways nearby. An exorcist from the church of St Nicholas of Myra was called in to help. Hundreds of people said that they witnessed the struggle between good and evil. In the dénouement, the ghost was banished to the bottom of the Red Sea, there to remain in chains until Judgement Day. Soon after, the priest collapsed and died. It was widely believed that laying a ghost could kill a man.

I was brought up on the edge of the weavers' quarters known as the Tenter Fields, where the Huguenots once stretched their cloth on tenterhooks. Up to the end of the forties the William and Mary houses built for the weavers were still standing, as was the Weavers' Hall. The houses bore traces of their former elegance, with simple doorways, high slender windows, solid staircases, wood-panelled rooms and gabled ends. In 1685, during the reign of Louis XIV of France, the Edict of Nantes (1598) which gave civil and religious liberties to Protestants was revoked. As a result thousands of weavers fled the country. A large group set up their looms in the prosperous district of the Coombe (the hollow or river valley of the underground river Poddle) in the Earl of Meath's Liberty. They were a closely knit community, distinguished by their colourful high wigs, and were responsible not only for silk-weaving but for the introduction of Irish poplin. Apprentices had to serve seven years. A story is told that one young man fell in love with his master's daughter and had the misfortune to get the girl with child. The pair were thrown out on the street to starve. The neighbours had a whip-round and got the couple enough money to make the exhausting journey to the New World, finally to settle in Pennsylvania and help found the city of Pittsburgh. They and their family prospered and, as in the old tales, lived happily ever after.

15

THE GHOSTS OF YESTERYEAR

I first met Maura Laverty in 1942 in the corridors of Radio Éireann, then housed at the top of the GPO in Dublin. The entrance to the radio station was in Henry Street and the lift that took one to the top creaked and groaned and got stuck between floors so often that it was nicknamed Jacob's Ladder. Maura was to become one of post-war Ireland's most popular writers – the Maeve Binchy of the fifties. She told her story in *Never No More* (1942), based on her life as a young girl in her grandmother's house in a little lost village on the edge of the Bog of Allen.

In Maura's youth Ballyderrig was as untouched by time as, say, Emily Bronte's Wuthering Heights. Only a few miles away from her home the wide plain of the Curragh of Kildare stretched out, with the redbrick military camp and an endless round of racing, parties, hunts, servants, flags, drums and glory. For the people of Ballyderrig, where barter was still practised and goods were paid for in eggs, butter and fowl, and where a child born out of wedlock was described as someone who had 'dropped from heaven', the Curragh with all its scandals, hard-

nosed glamour and excitements might have been a country on the far side of the moon.

From our first meeting Maura befriended me. She was
older, sophisticated, travelled and suspect. Her books, like
the works of Frank O'Connor, Kate O'Brien, Sean O'Faolain
and indeed almost every worthwhile author, had been
banned by the Irish censor. I was little more than a
schoolgirl when we first met. With all the ignorance and
arrogance of youth, and knowing nothing of writing, I had
submitted a forty-minute historical drama to Radio
Éireann and shortly after was booked for a six-month
series entitled *Ireland in Story and Song*. During the next
decade I wrote weekly dramatisations, as well as plays and
short stories for Radio Éireann and the BBC, and became
the friend and confidante of actors and actresses taking
part in my work.

My favourite was Siobhán McKenna, with her fund of
stage gossip and wicked wit. Her husband Denis O'Dea,
the Abbey actor, almost twenty years her senior, had all
the charm of the inveterate gambler. One evening over
supper with Siobhán at her home in Highfield Road,
Rathgar, Denis suddenly appeared in a dressing-gown to
share a bottle of champagne and regale us with stories
of Texan millionaires, gangsters from Las Vegas, as well
as the ordinary Joes he had come across in the casino
where he was employed professionally at the tables. Men
and women might win, but more often lose, a fortune on
the turn of a card or the spin of a wheel. Denis was a
wonderful mimic, though Siobhán said he wore her out
with his practical jokes.

Then there was Eithne Dunne, that talented actress,

married to the playwright Gerard Healy, who was dying of tuberculosis. She once told me that the time to dress up, paint your face and walk round as if you owned the town was when you hadn't a penny in your pocket. Pegg Monaghan was a favourite of mine, appearing in everything I wrote. Cyril and Maureen Cusack had frequent rows and made up in public. Bart Bastable fell for me for six months, during which time he listened to my woes, carried my parcels and treated me to meals he could ill afford. Joe Lynch had a fund of jokes and looked after me because he was friendly with my brother Seán, and the lovely gentle Christopher Casson played his harp, sang and acted as narrator to my stories and dramatisations.

The ghosts of all our yesteryears come flooding back: Denis Brennan, who was one of the most gifted actors I ever met; his wife Daphne Carroll; Rita O'Dea, who was an oculist and part-time actress and who gave us tickets for the Gaiety to see her brother Jimmy O'Dea in pantomime; Ginette Waddell, who introduced me to her aunt, Helen Waddell (1889–1965) the writer; Una Collins, fragile and temperamental, who died young; and many more. Writing for radio during those years was an extra source of income. Like the theatre folk I knew, I was generally hard-up, for we were paid a pittance at the Commission. The only one who could make ends meet was Séamus Delargy, who drew a modest salary from UCD where he was employed as lecturer in Irish. Much later he was appointed Professor of Irish Folklore, though he taught no students.

Maura once showed me a letter from Brendan Behan, which she carried in her purse for years. Brendan at the time of writing (1944) was a political prisoner and wrote from Cell 26, Arbour Hill Military Prison, thanking her for the great enjoyment she had given them with *Never No More*. Some of the inmates of the 'Hill' had clubbed together to buy the book and had taken it in turns to read it. 'And God help me, altho' I was last I had it longest,' Brendan concluded, urging Maura to continue the good work.

Years later, when Brendan had achieved immortality with *The Quare Fellow* (1954) and *Borstal Boy* (1958) and was described by English reviewers as a second Sean O'Casey, no one was more delighted than Maura, and when as a diabetic he wrecked himself with drink and begged money to quench his thirst, she gave him whatever she could spare. She was one of the warmest and most open-handed people I have ever met and had a small army of vagrants and down-and-outs whom she supported. She had no vanity about her looks but I always considered her one of the handsomest women in Dublin with her brown hair swept back in a French roll, clear skin and odd eyes, one grey and one with a brown tea-leaf, like Deirdre in the folktale, which was a sign of beauty.

Before meeting Maura, I had no interest in cooking. Then one evening she invited me to a charity midnight première of *Moulin Rouge* (1952), a film based on the life of Toulouse-Lautrec, in the Adelphi Cinema. She would expect me around six o'clock and give me a meal in her home in Leinster Road, opposite to where Lord and Lady Longford (of the Gate Theatre) had their townhouse. Delargy, as was his wont when I mentioned an important appointment, kept me working late, and the dinner was

ruined by the time I arrived. Maura was very understanding and whipped up a Spanish omelette, having
delegated me to run from cupboard to pantry fetching
eggs, vegetables and cheese. The meal was delicious, and
from that moment I became hooked on cooking.

Maura gave me a copy of her banned novel, *No More
than Human* (1944), the book that drew on her years in
Spain before the civil war. Girls of slender means from
all over Ireland flocked as governesses to Spain's great
houses and, at the age of seventeen, Maura joined their
ranks. 'It was funny,' she said, 'to hear the scions of the
Spanish nobility speak English with thick Irish brogues
and the six-year-old heir to a dukedom complaining to his
Antrim governess, "Miss, thon boy's after takken me wee
ball" or the eight-year-old Marquess de Rio Tente giving
his sweater to Miss Barry of Cork with the complaint: "Will
oo keep an eye on dis, I'm dead out wid de heat".'

Maura soon found herself in trouble. She put on a
scarlet swimsuit to play beachball with a couple of male
admirers, unheard-of conduct for a Spanish governess of
the time, and was instantly sacked. Undeterred, she taught
herself shorthand and typing and made an unprecedented
leap into journalism. 'The revolutionary design that Spain
took in after years was shaped in *El Debate*, the newspaper I wrote for,' she said, 'but though I was in the very
middle of what went on I noticed nothing. People are like
blotting-paper. The more worthwhile kind will absorb
clearly the good black ink of intellectual impressions. The
cheaper kind smudge everything but the red ink of
emotion. I am the cheaper kind.'

Looking back in the mirror of memory, all she could

see were the eyes of one of her close friends, Juan Negrin, Spain's most talented cartoonist and a revolutionary, watching his beloved wife Consuelo slowly dying of tuberculosis; the desperate eyes of Maruja, the maid in the house where she lodged, brewing a tisane in the hope of procuring an abortion; the gentle ashamedness of Mama Antonia, whose son Maura coached in English, because she had never learned to read. Mama Antonia ran a successful cake shop in Madrid and had a willing pupil in Maura for her regional Spanish dishes. She had already been well tutored by a grandmother who was reckoned the best cook in County Kildare and whose head was a card-index file of traditional Irish dishes and amazing old herbal remedies. She lent me a bundle of the recipes which she afterwards published under the title of *Full and Plenty* (1960) and which for years was the *Mrs Beeton* of Ireland.

She was a regular visitor to the Commission's archives. We would swap stories and legends before she brought me across Stephen's Green to the Shelbourne for lunch. There Margaret Burke Sheridan (1889–1958), the great Mayo diva, might hum an aria from one of her successes under her breath. She was blonde and glamorous, wrapped either in furs or in floating silks. It was rumoured that an Italian whose overtures she had rejected had blown his brains out in a box in La Scala, Milan, while she was on stage and that after the tragedy she never sang in public again.

I never tired of listening to Maura's stories of the people of Ballyderrig, the fairy rath, and the haunted house on part of the rath. She would describe in great detail the 'live and dead' markets held in the town in the weeks before Christmas, where women from the surrounding countryside sold their birds either dead or alive and then spent the higgler money on clothes and Christmas shopping. She described the avenue leading to the mill where in early spring snowdrops and crocuses splotched the avenue's grassy border with white and purple and gold. Mr Leadbeater the miller, who was a Quaker, lent her books; his daughter, Miss Hope, gave her lemonade and fairy cakes on warm days, and pancakes sprinkled with sultanas and glasses of warm milk sweetened with honey and dusted with cinammon when winter came. She swore that a neighbour, who went by the name of the 'fairy boy' and had a store of ballads and songsheets and strange stories of people no one else ever saw, was born in a rath. She told of the excitement in the house when her grandmother decided it was time to kill a pig, how the neighbours came in to help and partake of a supper of freshly made black and white puddings, slices of crispy brown liver, juicy cuts of heart with savoury stuffing and pale green colcannon, light and fluffy as bogcotton and pregnant with good rich gravy.

In return I told her what she probably already knew: that a pig should never be killed unless there was an 'r' in the month, that in the counties of Mayo and Galway it was believed that the killing should take place under a full moon and that hams and bacon were delicious if cured in the smoke of green wood. She loved Christmas and all it stood for, but I wasn't surprised when one year, after a hectic December of writing and broadcasting to the women of Ireland telling them how to cook the

Christmas fare, she insisted that her husband Jim book the family into the Gresham Hotel where she wouldn't be asked to lift a finger and would be cosseted as she was in the old days with her grandmother in Derrymore House. She invited me to join them but I was needed at home.

As time went on, Maura became even more successful. She had turned her novel *Lift Up Your Gates* (1946) into the play *Liffey Lane*, depicting life in the Dublin slums, which was one of the great successes of the Edwards-Mac Liammóir company in 1951. She followed this with *Tolka Row* (1951) and *A Tree in the Crescent* (1952), showing the upward climb of the family. *Tolka Row* would in time be turned into RTÉ's highly successful first soap and it ran for years after Maura died.

You couldn't listen for any length of time to Maura without becoming interested in food, so whenever I had a spare moment I could be found exploring the manuscripts in our archives, as well as the early Irish literary sources and the legends and stories connected with food, to discover what our ancestors ate and drank. It took many years, with many interruptions, before my own book *Land of Milk and Honey* (1991) was finally published. I only regretted that Maura was not still around so that I could dedicate the work to her with love and gratitude. She died alone in her home in Rathfarnham in 1966 at the early age of fifty-nine, her family scattered, her marriage to her husband Jim in ruins. He was a journalist with the *Irish Times*, a charming man and a failed writer. One night he gave me a play of his to read which had as theme the confusion caused in a bank by decimal currency.

The dialogue was clever and witty, and as I remember, the plot was full of suspense. Maura did all in her power to get it produced but unfortunately it was written a decade and more before the changeover in currency actually took place. Jim's misfortune was that he was a man before his time.

I wrote Maura's obituary for the *Sunday Press,* which at the time had the largest circulation of any paper in Ireland. I could see her once more in that lost country of her youth, young and high-spirited, running along the road, past hedges heady with woodbine, to her grand-mother's house – Gran, whom she described as 'the purple bog, the ripe wheatfield, the budding trees in May, good food and songs and firelight and the rosary at night'; Gran, who had a welcome for her coming and a prayer for her going. Her daughter Barry wrote me a letter of thanks at the time. I think Maura would have been pleased with my effort.

16

THE DINGLE PENINSULA

Every summer for more than thirty years I visited the little Irish-speaking village of Dún Chaoin, or Dunquin as it is known in English, a ten-mile drive from Dingle. There is a little grove of trees at Baile an Ghoilín where Lord Ventry had his seat. Look well because, save for a solitary ash or fairy thorn, you will see no more trees until you pass that way again.

As always when I make this journey, I am bewitched by the wanton gold of ragwort, the lavish patches of purple heather and the profusion of fuchsia looking oddly exotic in this wild and rugged landscape. Gulls fly screaming over the bogs and if you are lucky you may catch a glimpse of a lone heron perched on one leg in a shallow stream. An occasional bungalow sits comfortably where a ruined cottage once crouched. Donkeys carrying their load of turf or seaweed, and creamery carts with cans rattling have long since been replaced by high-powered trucks and speeding cars. Yet the peninsula still retains the air of loneliness captured by a scribe when he noted down in the *Annals of the Four Masters*:

The age of Christ, 1582: The lowing of a cow or the voice of a ploughman could scarcely be heard from Dún Chaoin to Cashel in Munster.

Past Ventry, known as *Fionn-Trá* (the bright strand) in Gaelic, the road climbs its winding way. Ventry is remembered in folklore as the scene of a great battle between Daire Donn, the king of the western world, and the Fianna, a band of warriors devoted to the service of the high king, Cormac Mac Airt. According to the Irish annalists, they lived in the third century AD. Finn, their captain, was the wisest man in Ireland and the way he came by his knowledge is an oft-told tale. From time immemorial men had sought to catch the fabled salmon of knowledge that lived in a pool near the river Boyne. Then Finéigeas, a druid who was tutor to young Finn, succeeded. He carried the fish as carefully as a jewel in a basket made of osiers and gave it to Finn to cook. 'Touch not a morsel,' he warned, 'for whoever has the first taste will have all knowledge.' Finn promised and watched anxiously as the fish turned first to gold and then to bronze over an applewood fire. He noticed a blister on the salmon's skin which he pressed down with his thumb. In doing so he burned himself and instinctively stuck his thumb in his mouth to ease the pain. That innocent act gave him the first taste of the fish and with it the gift. Ever after that, when he wished to look into the future, he had only to suck on his thumb and all the knowledge he wished was his. It was said that under the leadership of Finn, the Fianna of Ireland came into their glory, and with his death their glory passed away.

The Fianna enjoyed hunting, fishing, swimming, hurling and football during the day, and singing and story-telling around campfires at night. Occasionally they engaged in skirmishes with foreign invaders and were always the victors. It was the kind of careless life that most boys and their elders can only dream about. Perhaps this is the reason their exploits lived on in the memories of ordinary people down to our own times.

Dr Robin Flower (1881–1946), the distinguished British historian and scholar, who spent long periods on the Blasket Islands, describes an extraordinary encounter he had one day, showing how far back the thread of memory can go. He was out walking when he came upon an old man digging potatoes in a field. They exchanged greetings and the old man, knowing of Flower's interest in the past, laid down his spade and began to recite Ossianic poetry. After a little while he changed from poetry to prose and told a lengthy tale of the adventures of Finn and his companions throughout the world. 'I listened spellbound,' Flower told Delargy later, 'and it came to me suddenly that there on the last inhabited piece of European land, looking out to the Atlantic horizon, I was hearing the oldest living tradition in the British Isles.'

Onwards the road meanders between Cruach Mhártain and the flat tableland of Sliabh an Iolair. On the summit of Cruach Mhártain is a cromlech called *Leaba Dhiarmada agus Gráinne* (Dermot and Gráinne's bed). '*Tóraigheacht Dhiarmada agus Gráinne*' ('The Pursuit of Diarmuid and Gráinne') is one of the best-known of the Finn cycle of tales and was woven into a play in Irish by Micheál Mac Liammóir in 1928 to open the Taibhdhearc in Galway. The story relates how the beautiful princess Gráinne puts *geasa* or bonds on Diarmaid Ó Duibhne, described as the handsomest man in Ireland, to save her from the attentions of Finn, a man old enough to be her grandfather. According to the legend, Dermot and Gráinne travelled through Ireland meeting many adventures, never eating more than one meal, or sleeping more than one night, in the same place. Here in this mountain cromlech the lovers rested. 'And here,' the legend goes, 'Dermot kept watch for Finn over the harbour of Dingle.'

A little farther along the road the cliffs break into the sea and across the sound lie the Blasket Islands, now hidden by sea mists, now green and lovely like some enchanted Tír na nÓg. Nearest is Beiginis, small and flat with Oileán na nÓg (the island of the young) lying under its flank, and there beyond is an tOileán Mór, the Great Blasket, screening from view Inis na Bró and Inisicíleáin, where the golden eagle once nested. To the right is Inis Tuaisceart, the northern island, and far out in the Atlantic the gull-haunted pyramid of the Tiaracht climbs stark and desolate. Here stood the lighthouse whose flashing beacon was the last sight of home that many Irish emigrants saw as their ship made its way across the Atlantic.

When I first got to know Dunquin it was a place apart, a huddle of houses seldom visited by the outside world. After the Second World War visitors began to drift down the peninsula. At the end of the sixties David Lean arrived to make the film *Ryan's Daughter* (1970) and the world and his wife discovered that particular corner of the country. The unit built a schoolhouse overlooking the Blaskets and created a mock village on top of the hill, known as *an Ceathrú* (the quarter). Before long the fishermen upturned their currachs (or *naomhóga* as they are called there) and cast their nets aside to accept roles as extras. They took the glamour of film-making in their stride, entertaining and being entertained by the 'stars'. Sarah Miles they classed a good-looking woman, John Mills the best storyteller of the unit, and Trevor Howard and Robert Mitchum as men who could match them drinking the Guinness which was laid on free in the mock village. Pound, one of the fishermen and a well known character, complained to me that the porter was flat owing to the altitude. He was given a few lines to say in the film and could be heard boasting nightly of his acting ability in Maurice Kavanagh's pub, known far and wide as 'Kruger's'.

Maurice (1894-1971) got the name 'Kruger' because of his literary ability. As a boy he was much impressed by a talk given by the local schoolmaster on the Boer War (1899-1902) and so wrote a poem in praise of Paul Kruger, the President of the Transvaal Republic. The poem was published in a local paper and young Maurice got half a crown for his work. The innocent pleasure he took in his fame made certain that the name stuck. He was a big man, a handy thing for the proprietor of an Irish pub to be, with a personality larger than life. He had spent years working at a variety of jobs in New York, Boston, Los Angeles and Chicago, but the only one he boasted about was his stint as a PR man, though the term wasn't in use then. More than once he hinted that he was engaged by the Mafia and indeed at times some of them may have been glad of his services. According to himself, he was the intimate of the guys and dolls of Manhattan, the mouthpiece of the bootleggers and hoods, and could have made his name and fortune as an actor in Hollywood. At times he sounded like a character from a Damon Runyon story.

He swore he was a friend of 'Scarface', Al Capone, when the gangster was America's most wanted man. He described Capone as a hard man, quick on the draw, with a ferocious temper, but generous to a fault. In the end Kruger grew tired of the excitement of his life – or maybe his luck ran out. Whatever the reason, he packed his bags, said goodbye to the hurlyburly of prohibition America and returned to the tranquillity of the place of his roots. With the money he had saved, he married his cousin Kate and opened a guesthouse and pub within sight of the Blaskets, where everyone danced half-sets on the sawdust floor, where the beer was excellent but the meals were a moveable feast. Like Grand Central Station in New York, Kruger's pub had the reputation of being a place where if you waited long enough you were bound to meet everyone you knew.

Denis O'Dea always enjoyed a visit to Kruger's, listening to yarns about the host's years in the States. The dining-room was hung with photographs signed 'With love to Kruger' from such luminaries as Lillian Gish, Greta Garbo and Marlene Dietrich. Only the oleograph of the Sacred Heart hanging over the mantelpiece had no inscription, an omission which O'Dea is said to have remedied one night when he removed the print from the frame and inscribed it: 'From Jesus Christ to Kruger'.

Another frequent visitor was Cyril Cusack. It was at

Kruger's invitation, or so he claimed, that Cyril proposed to Maureen Kealey. His part in the romance was probably no more than wishful thinking but, if my memory serves me right, the Cusacks did spend part of their honeymoon in his guesthouse. The night they arrived there were drinks for everyone on the house.

I paid many visits to the Great Blasket before the last of the islanders left there for ever in 1953. On this the ultimate shore of the old world a hardy community kept a bare foothold for centuries. This home of Gaelic life and storytelling was made famous by Thomas O'Crohan (1856-1937) in *The Islandman* (1929), by Maurice O'Sullivan (1904-50) in *Twenty Years A-Growing* (1933), and by Peig Sayers (1873-1958), queen of the island, in her biography, *Peig* (1936), and *Reflections* (1939) and, of course, by Robin Flower himself, who encouraged the islanders to record their memories and folklore. From the day Flower first came to the Blaskets in 1910, he became the islanders' favourite visitor and remained so until his death more than thirty years later.

On 17 January 1946 Delargy noted in his diary:

Gerard Murphy and his wife Mary phoned to tell me that Robin Flower had just died. It came as a great shock. His last words to me were about the Blaskets and how he longed to see them once again. He praised the work we were doing for the collection of Irish folklore, saying that it was the only thing worthwhile.

17

Life on the Blaskets

When I first set foot on the Great Blasket, only a handful
of people remained and these reminded me of the wild
geese poised for flight. A few would cross the three-mile
sound to the mainland but most were bound for America
to settle in the Irish ghettos. They knew little of Dublin
but could reel off names of streets and stores in Spring-
field or Holyoke, Massachusetts, places to which the
islanders had been emigrating since the time of the Great
Famine.

It was a heartbreak for them to leave the island they
loved, where, if life was an unending struggle for survival,
it was also rich in companionship. They were often
marooned for weeks at a time, with neither doctor nor
nurse to tend their illnesses, nor priest for spiritual needs.
Every crop had to be carefully husbanded, cattle were
scarce and fish the mainstay of their diet. A couple of
times I went out in currachs with fishermen when they
were putting out lobster pots. Four times a day the pots
were hauled in, each yielding two or three dozen of the
finest lobsters caught anywhere in the world. In the

course of my life I have eaten in some of the best restaurants in the world but never tasted the equal of the lobsters I ate in Molly O'Connor's guesthouse in Dunquin.

In fine weather there is no more beautiful place in the world than the Great Blasket with the sun beating down on the white strand and the sea calm. To the south Iveragh and the whole of Dingle Bay reaches out; Dunquin, three miles across the sound, lies under the protection of Mount Eagle; and away to the north jutting out into Smerwick Harbour is Dún an Óir, the Fort of Gold. This promontory is still remembered as the spot where the massacre of the Spanish-Italian papal force took place on 10 November 1580 when, after a three-day siege, Lord Grey, Elizabeth I's Lord Deputy, accompanied by Sir Walter Raleigh, put the garrison of 300 men to the sword. Dún an Óir is and always has been the most haunted spot on the peninsula. It is mentioned in Pierce Ferriter's 'Lament of Maurice Fitzgerald, Knight of Kerry', who died in France about 1642.

The Banshee of Dunquin
In sweet song did implore
To the spirit that watches
O'er dark Dún an Óir.

I had a strange, almost mystical experience at Dún an Óir, one November day when it seemed that, for no more than a heartbeat, time had changed and I was witnessing something that had taken place many centuries before. After an uphill climb I had seated myself on an outcrop. I was winded, thinking of nothing in particular, when I became conscious of a strange babble of tongues. Startled, I swung round and saw the desperate faces of dying men. I jumped to my feet, the world steadied itself once more and I realised that what I was hearing was the cry of seabirds – gulls, gannets, stormy petrels and cormorants – and that the faces that had put the fear of God in me were nothing more than seaweed and rock. Yet there was something eerie about the place, the lowering skies and the crash of the sea below. That evening back in Molly O'Connor's guesthouse, I checked the *History of Kerry*, and sure enough it was the anniversary of the massacre of Dún an Óir which had taken place 380 years before to the very day.

The first time I visited the Great Blasket I was sure I had met my end. Halfway across the treacherous sound one of the fishermen leaned too far overboard in an effort to recover an oar and fell into the water. In those days few fishermen could swim and the boat stood on end, almost capsizing, as his two companions struggled to rescue the drowning man. Soon all was well and the currach was running rapidly over the waves. The lifting prow of the boat turned to the islands and in a short while we came in sight of the long shore of sand known as an Trá Bán (the White Strand). It is a proof of how young and heedless I was at the time that I didn't worry about the return journey.

A couple of islanders were waiting to help and in the excitement of landing I paid little heed to the piper on the hill, though the haunting air he was playing stayed with me for the length of the day. As the boat turned on its axis and we found ourselves floating easily up to the slip under a great cliff, the figure was lost in the sea-mist. We climbed the steep face of the hill to the village, an irregular huddle of houses crouching down out of the wind showing their black tarred roofs, on top of which white fish were laid out to dry.

On a second visit I heard the music again, this time played on a fiddle by a young man whose people had originally come from Inisicíleáin. He said that the air was called '*Port na bPúcaí*' (the fairy tune) and that it was the islanders' favourite. It was first heard in mysterious circumstances on the night of an American wake (the farewell to departing emigrants). The boy's great-great-grandfather was playing a few jigs and reels to keep up the spirits of the islanders, when from over the roof of the house came the sound of music that would put light heels on the feet of the dead. Backwards and forwards the wandering air moved, now crystal-clear, now fading away, again bright and merry, until at last the fiddler had every note by heart. It was said that if you heard the fairy music played by a fiddler on Midsummer's Night the secret of Inisicíleáin would be revealed. But, alas, the family who inherited the fairy tune are now scattered to the four winds and all the magic has gone from the islands. And no: I never found out who the piper on my first morning on the island was, or if indeed it was a mortal man at all. And as for the haunting music! Was it nothing but the cry of the wind and the chatter of the waves below? But if that was the case, how was it that I recognised the fairy tune when I heard it played by a descendant of the fiddler of Inisicíleáin?

Few of the islanders owned as much as a cow and they

had little if any money, but they honoured the Irish tradition of hospitality. On the day we visited the Great Blasket we were invited into all seven of the inhabited houses to take strong tea, homemade bread and boiled eggs. Now I like my tea light and have never been particularly fond of soft-boiled eggs but it would have been the height of bad manners to refuse the food. I chewed and swallowed and smiled and complimented them on the freshness of the food, only hoping I could hold it down. Which I did until to my relief the stormy seas of the return journey allowed me to bring it back up again with the sympathy of the three islandmen plying the oars.

To this day I can recall the modest comfort of the houses on the island, with their raftered ceilings and open fires and the fragrant smell of turf smoke which I love above French perfume. Every kitchen contained the usual accoutrements: settle-bed and dresser filled with delph, as well as a couple of chairs made of woven straw. Walls were hung with religious pictures that had been purchased in Dingle. They showed garish reproductions of the Sacred Heart (Christ with a flaming heart) as well as various saints and martyrs wearing woebegone expressions. Their mediocrity was redeemed by beautiful pictures of Our Lady of Perpetual Succour, modelled on the Byzantine original and sold to the islanders by a travelling pedlar years before.

On that occasion I visited the island school, which had been closed down on 24 June 1941 when there were only three poor scholars 'left to run wild as rabbits'. Six years later benches were still stacked against the wall, the blackboard still hung by two pegs, and on the wall over the teacher's desk a yellowing picture of Éamon de Valera hung alongside the inevitable Sacred Heart. A couple of dog-eared calendars from Holyoke in the USA had pictures of girls in bonnets and flounces leaning over rustic gates and gazing into the sunset, while a posse of cowboys could be seen forever riding the range.

Mairéad Ní Chatháin, a pretty girl of sixteen years, proudly showed us a pair of red shoes which had just been delivered by the postman, who was also king of the island. They had been advertised in a newspaper some visitor had brought in. Mairéad fell in love with the red shoes and wrote off to Frawleys of Thomas Street, Dublin, the advertisers, enclosing the cost and stating the size. She would wear them on her journey to Holyoke where she hoped to join her brothers and sisters. Her mother was resigned to the parting. She never expected to see her children again but it was 'as God willed'.

What struck me most forcibly about the island was the absence of crime, allied to the islanders' strong belief in the hereafter and a devotion to the Virgin Mary. This despite the fact that there was no church and the islanders seldom saw a priest. However, like fisherfolk the world over, they were fatalists. Robin Flower in his classic *The Western Island* (1944) retells a well known tale that he heard on the island. Three men were out fishing when one glanced over the side of the boat and saw far below him three men walking along a road. He said nothing to his two companions but each time he looked the spectral figures beneath the waves were keeping pace with the boat. The next day the boat put out to sea again, a storm blew up and the fishermen were drowned. Asked why the

fishermen had not taken heed of the warning, the storyteller replied, 'Dhera, what good would there have been
in that! A fisherman must follow the sea and how can a
man escape the day of his death? We have only our time
and, young or old, a man must go when he is called' – a
philosophy echoed in Synge's *Riders to the Sea*, when
Maurya the island woman says of her drowned son:

> *Bartley will have a fine coffin out of the white*
> *boards, and a deep grave surely. What more can we*
> *want than that? No man at all can be living for ever,*
> *and we must be satisfied.*

The Commission was only a year in existence when
Seosamh Ó Dálaigh was appointed as full-time folklore
collector, work he was to continue until he returned to
national teaching in 1952. Seosamh, or Joe as we called
him, recorded nearly four hundred tales from Peig Sayers,
one of the great narrators of the wonder tales of Ireland.
Joe was a genial soul with fair curly hair and the sea-
washed eyes of the people of the peninsula. He was a
native of the district, his father Seán having been a
teacher before him in the school in Dunquin. In her
autobiography Peig was to write: 'Even though I'm an old
woman now, I'm proud to say that I was taught by Seán
Ó Dálaigh.'

Peig left the Great Blasket some years before the final
evacuation in 1953 to settle once again in her native
Dunquin. In her book she wrote of an early life of great
hardship. At the age of fourteen she was sent into
domestic service in Dingle but made great plans to

emigrate to America to find fame and fortune. Her biggest disappointment was when the passage money failed to materialise and she was forced to turn once again to service. Soon after, she was 'rescued', as she put it, by an arranged marriage with a handsome islandman, Pádraig Ó Guithín, with whom she fell madly in love at first sight. She made her home on the Great Blasket and bore him ten children, five of whom died young. Tragedy struck again with the death of her dearly loved teenage son, Tomás, who fell from a cliff to the rocks beneath while out gathering heather with his friends. With no one in the house but a seriously ill husband, she prepared the battered and broken body for burial. Afterwards she was to write poignantly of that day:

I needed a heart of stone to be able to do it but I did. I put the statue of the Virgin on the floor beside me and from that moment forward I was but an instrument in her hands and in the hands of her Son.

When Seosamh Ó Dálaigh first introduced me to Peig, she was in her seventies, an old woman with a face scarcely lined, dark expressive eyes and hands, and a wonderful voice. Listening to her I thought that in another place and time she might have made her name as a great actress. In looks, gesture and timbre of voice she reminded me of our own Sarah Bernhardt, the inimitable and never-to-be-forgotten Siobhán McKenna. Ó Dálaigh, in the introduction to Peig's *Reflections,* says:

I wish I had the ability to describe the scene in her home in Dunquin on a winter's night when the stage was set for a night of storytelling. The evening meal was over, the day's work done, the family rosary finished. Over the hearth glowed a small peat fire and on the side wall an oil lamp gave a dim light. Peig was to be found like all storytellers in the place of honour on a low chair in front of the fire (unusual in the locality where women seated themselves by the hob).

I have my own memories of Peig. From our first meeting I found her matter-of-fact though friendly. It was clear to me from the start that she was a man's woman. If I were alone with her, we gossiped about everyday matters: the fishing, what visitors had arrived, the cost of living, how the hens were laying, whether the weather would hold. But let a man cross the door and her face changed, her eyes lit up. The male visitor was given a beaming smile, urged to stir up the fire, offered a drop of whiskey or a fill of tobacco, for Peig liked company when she smoked her pipe. Thus fortified, she flirted with each man as he arrived until the room was filled with neighbours and visitors whom she would entertain with a night's storytelling.

Sitting enraptured, observing the flash of her eyes or the way she clapped her hands or pointed over her shoulder at some dramatic point in the story, it crossed my mind that she might have been any old woman who had lived most of her life on an isolated island, but for a fortunate accident of birth. She had been born into a famous storytelling family and, unusually for a woman, had inherited the gift. She had met writers and scholars,

strength to pare the hard plug she loved. The medical staff were understanding; her days were numbered, there was no hope of recovery. She might as well enjoy the short time she had left. Her sightless eyes filled with tears on our last visit as she bade us goodbye and kissed Kevin's hand. I cannot remember her words to me. I'm sure they were gentle but as I have already said it was men she loved and, to give them their due, they loved her. She died in 1958 in Dingle hospital and with her went one of the last links of an older and more aristocratic civilisation.

Each summer a team of divers came over from Liverpool to search the Blasket Sound for Spanish gold. They stayed in O'Connor's guesthouse where Molly, the handsomest woman on the peninsula, was a superb hostess and cook. She had an infectious laugh and spoke rapidly in beautiful Irish. In its early days Bord Fáilte used a picture of Molly making a churn of butter on a postcard in the 'Discover Ireland' series. If Molly was known for her raven hair, dark eyes and good looks, her mother might have come out of a Velázquez painting. There was little doubt that a strong Spanish influence could be traced in the people of the Dingle peninsula, not surprising given the links that had been forged with Spain through the centuries. A story is told that in the olden days a woman went to her neighbour to borrow a cloak and got the response: 'No. I'm just slipping across to Spain to spend a few days with my husband's people.'

For many centuries there was a brisk smuggling trade in Spanish wine and wool, and it was customary for Spanish ships to run for shelter to the sound in the face of storms. The most dramatic encounter and the one that has lived longest in folk memory is that of the Spanish Armada. In the summer of 1588 the survivors of the ill-fated ships sent to destroy the power of Elizabeth I, limped east from the English Channel, many to try to find their way around the west coast of Ireland. On 15 September two great galleons sought shelter between the Great Blasket and Beiginis. For seven days they rode at anchor until they were joined by the *Santa Maria de la Rosa* which struck Stromboli Rock under the cliffs and sank, only one man surviving. He was taken prisoner in Dingle town where he told a strange story of a king's son and a king's ransom in gold bullion that had gone down with the crew. Twenty tides and more than twenty tides must have washed ashore bodies of drowned Spaniards that stormy autumn, but of all those who perished only one stays in folk memory: the young Prince of Asculo, natural son of Philip II.

Don Tucker, a cheerful and agreeable engineer from Liverpool, led his team of divers each summer in search of the *Santa Maria de la Rosa* under the waters of the sound. We all became firm friends and, though they brought up cannons and guns – and sea-urchins to keep us happy – the gold is still there. Near the schoolhouse in Dunquin you may see a grave which the people call *Uaigh Mac Rí na Spáinne* (the grave of the king of Spain's son). They say his spirit haunts the place and that only when Ireland is finally at peace will the treasure be found; and the ship will rise from the bed of the ocean to ride the seas in triumph once more.

18

THE MAYPOLE

After the return of the dead at dawn on the winter solstice
in the great pagan burial chambers in the Boyne valley,
our ancestors celebrated the coming of spring and summer by lighting bonfires on the hills and by gathering
flowers (and fruit in season). This delightful custom lasted
right down to our own times. Primroses, cowslips, butter-
cups, daffodils, marigolds and furze were picked before
dawn on May Day, strewn on the threshold and on the
floors of the house, laid on windowsills and hung over
the lintel for good luck.

In the Irish calendar May Day was regarded as the
beginning of summer, a day of enchantment when the
fairy folk were at their most active and magic was most
potent. Twice a year the people of the *Sí* changed residence, occupying summer quarters on May Day and winter
ones on November Eve. As they swept past in the *sí-
gaoithe* (the fairy wind that blows without warning) they
were apt, as we have seen, to abduct a young bride or a
child and leave a changeling in place of the stolen human.
Witches assumed the shape of hares, and ill-disposed

persons, by means of spells and incantations, stole their neighbours' milk and butter. Folk stayed up all night on May Eve and at dawn drove their cattle through the embers of the bonfires that had illuminated the night hills so that the animals might not be spellbound.

It was the custom in many parts of the country to decorate a maypole with ribbons and a May bush with egg-shells left over from Easter Sunday, to dance and light the obligatory fire. The Reverend Mr Beauford, an Anglican clergyman whose parish was Athy, County Limerick, has left an account of an elaborate dance that he witnessed on May Day 1787. Twenty-four couples, the girls elegantly dressed in white, their dresses decorated with ribbons made into the shape of roses, danced round a maypole and then circled the bonfire. In Dublin the two biggest and best-known maypoles were erected in Finglas, north of the city, and at Harold's Cross in the south. Sir William Wilde, in his *Irish Popular Superstitions* (1852), describes the dance at Harold's Cross on the road to Rathfarnham. Beside the maypole a great fire was lit which could be seen as far away as the Liberties on one side and the Dublin Mountains on the other.

There is scarcely a parish in Ireland in which in former times the feast day of the local patron saint was not celebrated with a 'pattern'. These celebrations took place in the ruins of a local church or monastery, by a lake or more often a 'holy' well named for the saint, in whose honour people did the 'rounds', reciting prayers. Part of the ceremony consisted of the drinking of well water or bathing afflicted parts of the body in the expectation of a cure. Different shrines were famed for the cures of different ailments. It was usual for pilgrims to leave tokens of their visit: money, a ribbon, a comb, a rag or, in the case of certain miraculous cures, a crutch or stick.

People brought along food and drink to patterns and fairs, and ended the day with music, dancing and occasionally faction fights. The patterns at Glendalough and Donnybrook were once the social highlights of the year for ordinary folk and were captured on canvas by artists of the last century. A time came when both patterns were attacked by the civil authorities and the clergy as occasions of riotous behaviour, drunkenness, debauchery and faction-fighting. The result was that by the beginning of the twentieth century they were nothing more than a folk memory.

Happily, maypole dancing was revived by Lady Aberdeen in the beautiful and extensive Iveagh Gardens. She was a remarkable woman, patron and foundress of the Child Welfare Guilds of the pre-social-welfare days of the 1920s and 1930s. These Baby Clubs, as they were known, did Trojan service for the mothers and children of Dublin's slums at a time when infant mortality was our shame. Maypoles were erected in the hollow of the Iveagh grounds, various clubs competed for prizes, and youngsters with nimble feet danced round the poles plaiting them with ribbons in rainbow colours. Cups and medals were awarded to the most skilful team of dancers, the most colourful maypole and the best guild. Bands played popular tunes in the best garden-party tradition. As a child I was taken to see the maypole fête and longed with all my heart to take part in the dance. In an effort to distract me, my mother handed me over to her friend Dr

Kathleen Lynn (1874–1955). Kathleen Lynn was our family doctor, a severely dressed woman who always wore a suit, collar and tie, and cycled everywhere. It was a time when women doctors were rare and those few had continually to compete with the male establishment.

Despite her formidable appearance, she was kindness itself, a woman activist who had taken part in the Easter Rising, an anti-TB campaigner and founder of St Ultan's Hospital for the sick children of the poor. She believed in fresh air, maintained that children wore too many clothes and once peeled off and threw into the waste-paper basket the numerous woollens with which my mother had swathed me. That day at the maypole fête she allowed me to help her spread stiff white sheets over a long table and gave me a slice from an enormous barm-brack that Lady Gregory had sent from County Galway.

Lady Gregory, she informed me, lived in a big house in Coole, knew many fairy stories, had taught herself to speak Irish and was responsible for the Abbey Theatre, where, if I behaved myself, I might be taken to see a play. I wasn't all that interested in Lady Gregory nor in the promise of a treat sometime in the future, but I was distracted by the plates of sandwiches cut in triangles, the little iced cakes and the jugs of lemonade and bronze tea-urns that the members of the Baby Clubs would shortly consume.

It was only when I became a folklorist that I realised the debt we owed to Lady Gregory. She was one of the first to appreciate the wealth of tradition of the tenants and small farmers amongst whom she lived in Coole. She collected folktales and herbal medicines, and amassed a fund of information about the customs connected with births, marriages and deaths. It is a truth universally acknowledged, as Jane Austen might have observed, that fairies hate fire and iron. From reading the Grimms' *Fairy Tales* I was well versed in this aspect of fairy lore and enquired of Dr Lynn if the same were true of the *Sí*. She sat me on her knee and told me the following tale which she had had from the lips of Lady Gregory herself and which put my doubts at rest.

> *In the shadow of Slievenamon, the fairy mountain in Tipperary, is a cottage which was visited one night by three hags who said they had come to teach the young bride how to spin her wool. The girl was horrified, knowing that they were of the Other World and that she might never be rid of them. She took a pitcher and went down to the well on the pretence of fetching water, where a wise neighbour, hearing her plight, told her what she must do. She ran back to the house crying out, 'Tá Sliabh na mBan tré theine!' ('Slievenamon is on fire!'). At that the hags threw down the spinning-wheel and wool, and disappeared into the night screaming, 'Our children will burn!' Thankfully they were never seen again.*

Slievenamon, situated in the Golden Vale and 2364 feet high, overlooks five counties and has always been re- garded as a magic mountain. Finn MacCool lived there, as did Oisín and Oscar and fifty beautiful maidens who gave it its name, which means in English 'the mountain of women'. It is said that people who live around the foot of the mountain are touched by enchantment. In the closing years of the nineteenth century a young man who lived in Ballyvadlea, one of the villages at the mountain's foot, became convinced that his wife was a changeling and that the only way he could banish the fairy spirit and recover the wife he loved was by the ordeal of fire. So, with the help of some neighbours, he held the 'changeling' over the fire and the unfortunate woman was smothered to death by smoke. The young husband and nine neighbours were taken to Clonmel Gaol and tried for murder but the evidence was so conflicting and so bizarre (it was clear they lived in a fairy-haunted world) that they were treated leniently and soon afterwards set free.

The only other recorded case of burning to cast out a spirit took place in Kilkenny in the early fourteenth century when one Petronilla was burned at the stake on a charge of witchcraft. She was the maid of Dame Alice Kyteler whose son William Outlaw was mayor of the city. Dame Alice escaped to Wales where she continued her activities. In Kilkenny today you may eat and drink at the Kyteler Inn and perhaps see the ghost of Dame Alice and hear her chanting her best-remembered spell: 'To the house of William my son, hie all the dust of Kilkenny town.' Each morning she was out before the dawn, sweeping the streets and turning all she gathered into gold. It was said that when the merchants and goldsmiths of Kilkenny went to inspect their treasures, all they found was dust.

Biddy Early from Feakle in County Clare, a famous clairvoyant and faith-healer, who was born around 1798 and lived into her seventies, was another character about whom Lady Gregory collected stories. Right up to the middle of the twentieth century, accounts of Biddy Early's doings still circulated through Munster and Connacht. She was a strong-minded woman who had buried four husbands and, like Chaucer's Wife of Bath, was on the lookout for a replacement when she died. People came from far and near for Biddy's cures. She claimed to have derived her knowledge from the fairies to whose forts she was said to travel great distances at night and who had given her a dark blue bottle from which she doled out medication. She had an unrivalled knowledge of herbal medicines and in addition could cure pains and aches by manipulation and the laying on of hands. She never used her power except for good and never took payment. She went to her grave a poor woman.

A humorous anecdote claims that an officious priest upbraided Biddy for dabbling in magic. She refused to 'mend her ways' and he left in high dudgeon, only to discover that his horse refused to budge. He was forced to seek Biddy's help with the recalcitrant animal. She whispered something in the horse's ear, whereupon the animal whinnied a reply and took its master home safely. She wasn't to be left in peace; she was 'read from the pulpit' by the local clergy, who thundered that people who visited her were in danger of damnation. However, this had little effect on her popularity with those in sore need of relief. After her death, the men of the cloth had their revenge when the local priest threw the famous blue bottle into Kilbarron Lake. Several people risked at least pneumonia, if not drowning, in attempts to recover the bottle. It was never found and Biddy took her skills and knowledge of herbs with her to the grave.

The third member of the trio who had such an effect on the Irish theatre was John Millington Synge. Yeats, who met him in Paris in 1896, claimed that he advised the dark-haired Dubliner, who was trying to make a name in literature using French models, to leave the city and go to the Aran Islands. 'Live there as if you were one of the people; express a life that has never found expression,' he recommended. This Synge did with sensational results. *Riders to the Sea*, which has been described as the best one-act tragedy in the English language, was based on a story Synge heard in which the battered body of a drowned fisherman washed up near his home on the Aran Islands is recognised by the clothes he wore. Fishing families along the western seaboard had their own traditional knitting patterns handed down from mother to daughter. Often the only way the townland or village of the drowned man could be identified was by the stitches used in the sweater he wore. Fisherfolk reading the pattern would send the body home, even hundreds of miles away, so that it could be buried in the family grave.

Synge was never as intimate with Lady Gregory as Yeats and visited Coole only five times, but it is certain that without him and his plays the Abbey would not have had its great renown. His first success, *In the Shadow of the Glen* (1903), was based on a story told to Synge by Pat Dirane, a *seanchaí* of Inishmaan, one winter night in 1898. It is a blackly comic account: a Wicklow man, well-stricken in years, feigns death in order to entrap his young wife, who, he suspects, has fallen in love with a neighbouring farmer.

Of all Synge's plays the most famous is *The Playboy of the Western World* (1907), based upon another story Synge heard in Aran. It encapsulates the difference between a romantic tale and a dirty deed. At the opening of the play Christy Mahon is only a scared boy convinced he has killed his father but, because of the passion and colour with which he tells his story, he dazzles not only the young Pegeen Mike but the experienced Widow Quin. He goes on to become the hero of the hamlet, winning the heart of Pegeen, as well as all the prizes at the sports. And though he finally falls from grace when his father comes back 'from the dead', he retains the heroic self-confidence his stories have given him, boasting, 'Ten thousand blessings upon all that's here, for you've turned me into a likely gaffer in the end of all, the way I'll go romancing through a romping lifetime from this hour to the dawning of the Judgement Day.'

Perhaps one of the most neglected of Anglo-Irish folklorists is Sir William Wilde. He was born in Castlerea in County Roscommon and became a distinguished eye and ear surgeon. He married Jane Francesca Elgee, 'Speranza' of *The Nation*, and was the father of Oscar Wilde. He spent his summers in a villa on the shores of Lough Corrib which he called 'Moytura' after two great mythical battles that were sited near there. While tending to the local people he wrote down their stories and legends. He would cross moor and mountain to treat poor sufferers blinded by smoke in windowless cabins. They would attempt to pay the 'great doctor' with gifts: a clutch of eggs, a fowl, a handknitted gansey or a length of tweed. Instead, he would bargain for a fairytale, a ghost story, an escapade of the Fianna or an account of an ancient god. *Irish Popular Superstitions*, his first collection, was dedicated to Speranza, who after his death published two further books of material he had collected: *Ancient Legends, Mystic Charms and Superstitions* (1888) and *Ancient Cures, Charms and Usages of Ireland* (1890).

The second battle of Moytura was a struggle between good and evil, fought between the beautiful *Tuatha de Danann* and the ill-favoured Fomorians. Long and hard the battle raged, says the old tale; great the slaughter and grave-lying that was there. Pride and shame were side by side and there was danger and indignation until the two gods, Lugh and Balor, met in single combat. An evil eye had Balor the Fomorian. The eye never opened save on a battlefield. It had a polished ring on its lid and it took four men to lift this lid. It had a poisonous power. If an army looked on that eye, though they were many thousand, they were doomed to die. As the lid was raised from Balor's eye, Lugh cast a slingstone which carried the eye through the back of the head, while his own army, in fear, looked away. And the slingstone and the eye fell on the host of the Fomorians and they were destroyed and the battle won by the *Tuatha de Danann*.

The concept of the evil eye is well known in Irish folklore and there is a belief that goes back to pre-Christian Ireland that great harm can come to anyone who is 'overlooked'. Severe punishments were meted out under the Brehon Laws to those who used the power of the evil eye to harm others. Oscar Wilde, who was very superstitious, believed in the evil eye, and during his trial and incarceration in Reading Gaol was convinced that at some time in his life he had been 'overlooked'. The early wonder tales he heard in Moytura, the stories of the people of the Other World, with their love of dancing, music and fine clothes and their dedication to a life of pleasure, influenced the marvellous stories he wrote for children; they may also have played a part in his hedonistic approach to life. In 1894, at the height of his fame, he would write: 'Superstitions are the colour elements of thought and romance. They are the opponents of common sense.' He encouraged the young Yeats, reviewing his work and praising his book *Irish Fairy and Folk Tales* (1888): 'It is delightful to come across a collection of purely imaginative work. Mr Yeats has a very quick instinct in finding out the best and most beautiful things in Irish folklore.' Oscar Wilde's son Vyvyan relates how their father kept himself and his brother Cyril enthralled with the folktales he had first heard as a ten-year-old, from Frank Houlihan, a Galway storyteller who worked as a handyman around 'Moytura'. A favourite bedtime story told of a great melancholy carp that lived at the bottom of Lough Corrib and that would rise to the surface only at the music of an ancient song. Oscar Wilde used to sing his children to sleep with the lullaby, '*Táim-se i m' chodladh is ná dúisigh mé*' ('I'm sleeping and don't waken me').

19

THE FARM BY LOUGH GUR

Set between the peasant class – maidservants and spailpíns, or landless men of the nineteenth century, who
travelled from one end of Ireland to the other or jour-
neyed across the seas in search of work – and the Anglo-
Irish, who lived a life apart in their 'Big Houses', were the
largely silent people, the tenant farmers. Many were
sturdy, honest and hard-working men with a passion for
land, who took little interest in politics but believed in
the old way of life. Some boasted, as did their poorer
neighbours, that they were descended from kings, bards
and storytellers, and who could deny their claims! One
of the most fascinating accounts of the life of a comfortable farming family is told in *The Farm by Lough Gur*
(1937) which is in fact the memoirs of Sissy O'Brien, the
daughter of the house. My maternal grandmother had
been at boarding-school with the same Sissy O'Brien in
Bruff, County Limerick. When the book was first published
my grandmother gave me a copy and said that it was
'required reading' for a girl brought up in Dublin. To say
I enjoyed it would be an understatement. I didn't leave it

out of my hands until I reached the last page.

Two books of my youth were to have a profound effect on the career I would follow: the Grimms' *Fairy Tales* and Sissy O'Brien's story. Mary Carbery (who wrote the book from Sissy's recollections of her young days) was seeking the words of a lost folk song in Bruff in the summer of 1904 when she met a Mrs Fogarty, who was an enthusiast for the old stories and legends of Bruff and Lough Gur. Mrs Fogarty was the Sissy O'Brien who had been reared in Lough Gur, the daughter of a successful tenant farmer, John O'Brien, who rented his land from a kind and considerate landlord, Count de Salis. Sissy had never kept a diary but had a phenomenal memory. The book that resulted was a labour of love for narrator and scribe.

There were tales of the banshee Áine whose fairy music, the *ceolsí*, comforted the dying and their families, and of Fer Fí, the red-haired dwarf who played three tunes on his three-stringed harp: sorrow, sleep and happiness. It was lucky to hear Fer Fí laughing. The O'Brien children, like their neighbours, knew that the fairies lived in hollow hills and that a drowned city lay beneath the waters of Lough Gur. Sissy recalls superstitions and tales of giants, ghosts, holy wells, and fairy thorns, which she had learned from the maids in her mother's dairy.

There is more to the book than old superstitions and beliefs. Though set in the nineteenth century, it covers a much wider canvas. There is an account of an old woman called Moll Ryan who remembered her father and the neighbours cheering at the death of William of Orange in 1702. A street trader in Moore Street told me a similar story one day in the late 1940s as I left Radio Éireann.

She said that the people of the Liberties held a mock wake when they heard the news and drank to King William's perdition in whiskey and porter. There are folk memories of the Great Famine and the Fenians and an account of Sissy's meeting with Charles Stewart Parnell, who looked tired and pale and before whom she and her sister Bessie secretly agreed to genuflect as they did in church. Before they could do so, he turned away, to the relief of their mother who scolded the girls for trying to make a spectacle of themselves.

Little was known in the O'Brien household of the Irish language or of Irish literature, but the works of Dickens and Thackeray were read by John O'Brien to his family and any of the neighbours who happened by. What was lacking of Irish literature was compensated for by the folktales, charms and legends that coloured their lives. The countryside around is dominated by the awesome Lough Gur. Tradition has it that every seven years the lake demands the heart of a human being and that Garret, Earl of Desmond, is doomed to gallop over the surface of the waters riding a milk-white horse with silver shoes. The belief is that he must continue to ride until the silver shoes are worn out. Then he will be loosed from the enchantment which binds him and live a man among men since he never died.

Like most of the farming class of the time, the O'Brien household was Spartan, self-contained and happy. The household rose early and the maids and farmboys sat down to a breakfast of stirabout (porridge) and plenty of milk, bread and potatoes. Dinner at midday consisted of milk, potatoes and bacon, with maybe a helping of pork if a pig had been killed. At four o'clock buttermilk or tea and bread and butter were taken out to the men working in the fields. Supper consisted of bread, milk and porridge. The maids had the same food as the family but at different times, the only exception being that the master of the house had two boiled duck eggs and the mistress a hen egg.

Up to the advent of radio and television the monotony of life on many Irish farms was broken by callers: neighbours would visit a particular house to play cards or exchange news, gossip and stories. Beggars were welcomed with food and old clothes and were given help to bury their dead. A long-nosed spinning-woman came to Lough Gur whenever the sheep were shorn and the wool gathered, and there was always the travelling tailor. Occasionally a pedlar might call with a basket of ribbons, coloured handkerchiefs, cheap jewellery, tapes and cotton. Tinkers or tinsmiths, as the travelling people were then known, mended pots and pans, milk-cans and basins, or exchanged ones they had made earlier for food and the loan of a field to graze their horses and, if times were good, the occasional silver shilling.

A couple of times a year a dancing-master called. Then the piper carefully undid the bundle of straw and rags to reveal his pipes tenderly wrapped in red silk. After a few preliminary wails while the pipes were being prepared, a quadrille started the dancing; this was followed by reels, jigs and hornpipes, winding up with the Sir Roger de Coverley. Another musical visitor to the house was a fine violinist, always known as Mr Regan. His pride had been sorely wounded in one of the Ascendancy houses when, hoping to give the titled owners and their guests a treat, he played Mozart's Adagio in D. 'You would think,' he afterwards complained, 'that the exquisite air would enthral any mortal man or woman, let alone the cultivated nobility. But instead his lordship shouted, "Oh, Regan, do stop that and give us the Fox Chase", and the company roared after him, "Yes, yes, the Fox Chase", and her ladyship clapped.'

If bards and storytellers were welcome to every hearth, the same was true of the ordinary traveller. The Irish are by nature gregarious and fond of alcohol; it was never a hardship on even the poorest to entertain guests. Tourists, travel writers and even the unwelcome settlers noted this characteristic time and again. Fynes Moryson, who came to Ireland as Lord Deputy Mountjoy's secretary in 1600 and remained with him through the long and bitter campaign that led to the defeat of Hugh O'Neill, kept a record of his time in Ireland. In it he wrote, 'The common Irish like to spend money freely. Whenever they come to a market town to sell a cow or a horse, they will never return home until they have drunk the price in Spanish wine which they call "the King of Spain's daughter".' He had no great love for the Irish, as may be gathered, but even he credited Irish whiskey as 'the best drink in the world', a judgement with which, as we have already noted, Elizabeth I concurred.

It was considered important to welcome and invite in any caller to the door; the custom of hospitality was no myth but a living tradition. The greatest dishonour a person could bring upon himself was to be accused of being tight-fisted or miserly. Inns and hostels were free to all comers, their upkeep paid for by the hosteller, a man of means but not of the first importance, who sought to buy his way into aristocratic society by the lavishness of his hospitality. Even in modest houses it was taken badly if a visitor went away empty-handed or hungry. 'Is it leave with the curse of the house on you!' was cried if food or help were refused.

It wasn't only English travellers who were taken by the extravagant hospitality and conviviality of the peasant class, but the often feckless Anglo-Irish. In this as in other respects they took their colour from the native Irish and many kept up a continuous round of house parties with kitchens thronged with musicians, storytellers, itinerant tradesmen, spailpíns and beggars. The lord of the manor might be reduced to putting his boon companions up in the henhouse but prided himself on the fact that no one was ever turned away. It is in the nature of things that all must come to an end, and customs and traditions that had survived the odds for three or four thousand years were swept away by the Great Famine of 1845–47. It wasn't that the Irish would refuse to share their last potato with a hungry visitor; they were afraid to open the door to the dread spectre of the famine fever. Never again would unstinted and prodigal hospitality be taken for granted.

20

THE GREAT FAMINE

In 1945, one hundred years after the potato blight struck Ireland, the Irish Folklore Commission issued a questionnaire, *The Famine of 1845-47*, and received a larger response than any questionnaire issued before or since. Over five hundred people from all over Ireland sent harrowing accounts of what was remembered in family lore and in the folklore of the neighbourhood. Over and over again tribute was paid to the Society of Friends (or Quakers as they are popularly known) who worked ceaselessly to feed the starving and nurse the dying. Even when everyone else had given up in despair, they laboured on, and when in 1849 they finally abandoned relief work, Ireland had lost her most valuable friends.

The summer of 1845 had been a halcyon one. A bumper potato crop was expected. Then, in August, with appalling suddenness the blight struck Ireland. This was a disease which had manifested itself in America the year before and was carried back to Ireland - in ships, by vermin or by migrant birds. No one knew. On the eve of the Great Famine Ireland's population was reaching nine million. In the decade that followed, that number would be halved, millions would be swept away either to paupers' graves or on the 'coffin' ships bound for America and Canada. A commissioner of emigration in the United States wrote poignantly at the time:

If crosses and tombs could be erected on the waters . . .
the whole route of the emigrant vessels from Europe
to America would long since have assumed the
appearance of a crowded cemetery.

Gone too was an older way of life. Now every door was closed to traveller and beggar because of fear of the fever which killed more than famine. Down the centuries the Irish had been noted for their gaiety, courage, optimism and love of their native place. When the hunger came they fled in their millions and for those who remained life would never be the same again.

Over the years the offices of the Commission were visited by writers and scholars – and people with no particular axe to grind, just curious about what went on there. There was Gerard Healy, actor, playwright and husband of Eithne Dunne, the beautiful actress who rivalled Vivien Leigh in looks and talent. Gerry had a great-uncle who had lived through those terrible times and told him stories as a boy that had haunted him. He spent many weeks trawling through questionnaire replies and the information gathered by our full-time collectors. The result was the first Irish Famine play, *The Dark Stranger*, with its haunting song-motif that I can still remember:

Oh! the praties they are small over here, over here.
Oh! the praties they are small over here.
Oh! the praties they are small and we digs them in
   the Fall
And we eats them skins and all, full of fear, full of
   fear.

The play, produced by the Edwards-Mac Liammóir company at the Gate in 1945, was an enormous success.
Micheál, in his theatrical autobiography *All for Hecuba*,
promised a great future for Gerry and Eithne. Even as
Gerry worked in our archives he already had tuberculosis.
I pretended not to notice his flushed face and sudden cold
sweats. In the end he succumbed to the disease, leaving
Eithne and a baby daughter. She, who had given one of
the best performances I have ever seen in the title role
of Brecht's play *Mother Courage*, emigrated to England
where for a time she had great success with the Bristol
Old Vic before her own untimely death.

Another visitor who became interested in what we
were doing at the time was David Thomson, who later
produced a series of great documentaries for the BBC and
wrote several books, among them the classic *Woodbrook*
(1974). Meeting David was the beginning of a friendship
that ended only with his death. He was a tall, gangly man
who had all but lost his sight as a child and ever after
wore 'bottle' glasses. Even as a young man he had a total
disregard for the clothes he wore. Indeed, in later life he
could be seen in a kind of brown outfit which was too
big and baggy and put me in mind of nothing so much
as a Franciscan habit. He was reared a Protestant but I

doubt if he had any religious beliefs. Like Francis of Assisi, he had a wonderful way with old people, children, birds and animals, as well as having the most seductive voice. I can truly say he was the gentlest, most unworldly person I was ever to meet.

In 1932 David, then eighteen years old and a history student at Oxford, came for the first time to Woodbrook in County Roscommon, thirty miles from Sligo. He was employed for the summer to tutor Major Kirkwood's two daughters, the four-year-old Tony and Phoebe, who was twelve. The Kirkwoods were an Anglo-Irish family whose ancestors had been settled in Ireland on 'planted' lands since the 1641 Irish rebellion. In the three hundred years that had elapsed the Kirkwoods, like many more of their kind, had never wavered in their allegiance to Britain.

When David first met the Kirkwood family they were 'on their last legs'. He worked with the major and the farmhands on and off for ten years. He had been turned down for military service in Britain because of his poor sight. By the time he left Ireland for good, the Kirkwoods were finished, the banks had foreclosed and the major was forced to sell off the bloodstock he had hoped would retrieve his fortune. The family said goodbye to the house they loved in spite of its leaking roof and rotted floors, and went to live with relatives in Dublin. David and Phoebe paid a last visit to their favourite spot, the Hill of Usna, where the legendary and ill-fated Deirdre and the sons of Usna had been treacherously killed by Conor Mac Nessa. This was in the days when the Celts were the planters and the native Irish had been defeated in battle. Those that were left hid in the woods and mountains.

According to legend, they acquired supernatural powers and in time became the fairy folk, the people of the *Sí.*

By the end of the war the nature of Woodbrook had turned full circle. A local family, the Maxwells, who had worked for the Kirkwoods for generations and were looked on as old retainers, bought the house and the estate with the help of American money. They claimed that the land had originally been theirs before Cromwell and his followers dispossessed them. As too often happens, the dream was soured by reality. In June 1968 David paid a last visit to a now derelict Woodbrook to find that the place had become an albatross round the Maxwells' necks. The land lay fallow, the yard was neglected, windows broken, stables falling to bits. Most of the house had been left unoccupied for a quarter of a century while the Maxwells lived in what had been the servants' quarters. The estate was crippled by rates.

David often recalled his early years in Ireland and the love-hate that existed between the house and the local people. Major Kirkwood's way with the men and women who worked for him was casual and friendly, and though the servants got nothing except their keep and a payment at Christmas or on marriage, they did not resent their lot. The sins of the fathers were visited on the children; the major's forebears had regarded themselves not as settlers but as part of a garrison in a hostile land. This attitude and the difference in religion made mutual mistrust inevitable. The Maxwell family felt that they had more reason than their neighbours for resentment, though they were on the surface loyal and good workers. The Maxwells' particular trouble was that they carried a burden of guilt that they alone of all their friends and relations had survived the Famine. Old Mrs Maxwell, known in the family as Nanny, told David the story one day. Her parents had married very young, as was the custom then, and had a family before and during the Famine. 'It was the hand of God,' she said. 'What else would it be but the hand of God when a white mist came down over the whole of Ireland on a grand crop of potatoes, growing thick and strong and the flowers on them. And in the morning the whole country black with rotten stalks.'

Somehow her parents and some of the children survived the hunger, until near the end of the Famine her father persuaded her mother to take herself and the younger ones to the workhouse while he prepared the land for spring. But they were turned away, ill and starving. They had, however, escaped the cholera, and had hope. Without the land they would have porridge and no hope. It was then that the landlord, James Kirkwood, sent for Nanny's father and made a bargain that was worthy of Mephistopheles himself. He offered his starving tenant a house, food for himself and his family and a job as a herdsman – but at a price. 'Nearly half the houses in the townland were empty,' Nanny said, 'the people having died or the lucky ones gone to America. Even so, there were many that hoped for a crop the next year. But Mr Kirkwood had decided to clear the land and his idea was that my father would persuade the remaining tenants to go quietly when the military tumbled down their houses. My father stood on the roof,' the old woman continued, 'and threw down the roofs of his own uncles, his cousins and neighbours. In the teeming sleet and snow the evicted the Light Brigade – and of a life of Florence Nightingale. Apart from that we knew little. She was not a woman to engage in light gossip or confidential chat. She was probably in her early forties but it was difficult to pinpoint her age. She dressed mainly in sober colours, black, white or grey, wore her hair swept neatly back and had the impeccable good manners of the well-bred Englishwoman. I worked alongside her for a year but never really got to know her. She was certainly an object lesson in how to go about writing a book.

She would arrive each morning on the dot of 9.30 and did not leave until we closed eight hours later. She usually had an apple or a piece of cheese for lunch, taken at her desk, and she sometimes asked permission to work late. In the end we gave her the use of a key; it seemed the polite thing to do. She seldom bothered us except for a translation of a piece of Irish in one of the manuscripts or to ask our librarian, Dr Thomas Wall, to help her find a passage in a particular book. Now and again she would visit Trinity College to consult the Junior Dean, Dr R. B. McDowell, or take time off to meet Quakers at the Society of Friends in Eustace Street. Otherwise it was the State Papers Office in Dublin Castle or the History Department in UCD in Earlsfort Terrace where the Professor of Modern History, Dr Dudley Edwards, gave of his time and expertise. He was something of a character and she liked his wit. Once I walked into my office to find him stretched out full length on the floor. I was sure he had taken a sudden and fatal heart attack and I was about to ring for an ambulance, when he got to his feet, nonchalantly brushing himself down. When I scolded him for giving me

such a fright, he said that he usually took a nap at that
hour of the day on the most convenient floor.

Apart from the time she spent either at the Commission's office or in the reading room of the National
Library, Ms Woodham-Smith appeared to closet herself in
the penthouse she occupied in the Gresham Hotel during
her stay in Dublin. Once I invited her to see an O'Casey
play at the Abbey Theatre but she said there just was not
time. Then, on a summer's day in 1960, she wiped her
tired eyes, shoved another few sheets of paper into her
already bulging briefcase, thanked us all and bade us
goodbye, promising to return when her book was finished.
When *The Great Hunger* was published in London in 1962,
it caused a furore. It relentlessly charts the course of the
Famine and the *laissez-faire* attitude of the British government. One of the most moving passages in the book is
taken from a letter written by Father Mathew (1790–1856),
the apostle of temperance, to the head of the Treasury,
Charles Edward Trevelyan:

*In the month of July [1846] I passed from Cork to
Dublin and this doomed plant bloomed in all the
luxuriance of an abundant harvest. Returning on the
third instant I beheld with sorrow one wide waste
of putrefying vegetation. In many places the wretch-
ed people were seated on the fences of their decaying gardens, wringing their hands and wailing
bitterly the destruction that had left them foodless.*

Ms Woodham-Smith came to Dublin to present each
member of the staff with a signed copy of her book. With

the help of Toddy O'Sullivan, at that time manager of the Gresham and one of the best-known hoteliers in Dublin, she threw a party in the penthouse. Wearing a stunning black and gold cocktail dress and gold earrings, she greeted each of us with a hug and a kiss. She looked a different woman.

The dust jacket she had chosen for her book was a dramatic painting in oils by Lady Butler of an eviction scene of the Great Famine. In the foreground is the stark figure of a handsome woman in peasant garb standing outside her roofless cottage in Glendalough, while the battering-ram party can been seen moving off in the distance. A year later Cecil Woodham-Smith would present the Irish Folklore Commission with a Famine picture she had bought in Christies. It is an oil painting by Daniel MacDonald: a horrifying depiction of ragged, desperate men and women, entitled *Irish Peasants Discovering the Blight in their Potato Store*. Both this and *Eviction* can be seen hanging on the walls of the Department of Irish Folklore, at University College, Belfield.

21

WILD GOOSE LODGE

I had dithered too long, arriving late in Jammets restaurant to keep a date with Patrick Kavanagh, who was the foremost and most eccentric poet of the fifties. He was drinking in the bar with the writer District-Justice Donagh MacDonagh and his wife Nuala. Nuala Smith was Donagh's sister-in-law and second wife. The Smiths were neighbours of mine who lived in Lullymore Terrace at Sally's Bridge, overlooking the Grand Canal. On Sunday nights they kept open house and played cards. Nuala taught me to play poker on the bus coming home from school. I admired her style. She had a husky voice, moved in arty circles and employed the services of a theatrical dressmaker. When she gave up wearing school uniform and went to work in the civil service, instead of the usual twinsets and tweed skirts she appeared in witches' hats and flowing cloaks over low-cut dresses of black linen or red wool. Her wardrobe was uncluttered. When she acquired a new outfit, she wore it day in, day out, until it lost its novelty. Then she threw it into the nearest bin.

On the night before her wedding to Donagh, she took

me backstage to a party in the Abbey. For a dare she wore her wedding dress, in white wool, embroidered with a Celtic motif. During the night someone accidentally spilled a glass of porter over the dress. Next morning Nuala walked confidently up to the altar in her scarlet going-away suit. Scarlet was not in those years regarded as a suitable nuptial colour but both the MacDonaghs and the Smiths believed in the bohemian life.

I knew little of the MacDonagh family history, though I suspected that at some time they must have been 'overlooked'. Few of them died in their beds. Donagh's father Thomas, academic, poet, dramatist and revolutionary, was executed by firing-squad in Kilmainham Gaol on 3 May 1916, after the Easter Rising. A few years later Donagh's mother was drowned while swimming in the Irish Sea. His first wife, Nuala's sister, took a seizure in her bath and died before anyone could get to her. Some years after Donagh's early and sudden death of pneumonia, Nuala herself choked on a chicken bone in her home in Sandymount and was dead on admittance to hospital. She was still as striking as she had been in her youth.

That evening in Jammets I begged the MacDonaghs to join us for dinner but they hastily made their excuses, leaving me to trail into the dining-room with a man who had the reputation of being moody, if not downright rude. You may well ask what in heaven's name I was doing with a poet, poor as a church mouse, dining in the most exclusive restaurant in town, with its French menu, starched white table linen, po-faced waiters and well-heeled clientele. A couple of days earlier when I was eating shepherd's pie in the Country Shop, a restaurant on St Stephen's Green then frequented by minor civil servants, struggling artists and farmers' wives up for a day's shopping, I had been joined by Paddy Kavanagh and asked for a date. He said he had money to spare, and as proof of good faith showed me a cheque for £100 (no mean sum in those days) which he had received from his publisher, to whom he said he had sold the rights of his novel *Tarry Flynn* (1948).

Our conversation in Jammets got off to a bad start. Kavanagh looked spruce enough but he had taken a few drinks and was inclined to sulk. However, by the time we got to the duck and trimmings, things were looking up. The conversation had taken a literary turn and Paddy was discussing seventeenth-century poetry. The only poet of the period I could remember was Andrew Marvell. 'To His Coy Mistress' had been the favourite of the English class at our convent school and we shivered and giggled when the nun who taught us recited the lines

The Grave's a fine and private place,
But none I think do there embrace.

To keep up my end, I endeavoured to imitate Sister John the Baptist's sepulchral tones. Paddy's response took my breath away. 'If you become my mistress,' he solemnly declared, 'I shall write an ode to you, and your name will be forever enshrined in the poetry of the twentieth century.' I often wonder whether he had a poem like 'Raglan Road' in mind when he made this offer.

Earlier on, at the entrée stage, Paddy had enquired as

to my financial prospects. If I had any money or expectations, he said, he would like to marry me. He deserved the truth, so I laid my cards on the table: I had no expectations great or small and no money beyond my salary which amounted to £4 a week and the little I made writing scripts for Radio Éireann, an income that might cease at any time. Secretly I hoped he had not gambled away his royalties since issuing the invitation. Otherwise I could see myself washing dishes to pay for the meal. I boasted that I had wealthy relations sure enough, but since our family were not on speaking terms with them, it was highly unlikely that any money could be expected to come our way from that quarter. As for my parents, seeing the shifts to which they were put to feed and educate their brood, they were unlikely to leave more than the price of their coffins.

Paddy said he understood poverty only too well but that it was a poet's duty to marry money, adding kindly that a poet's girl should be well-bred, convent-educated, wrapped in middle-class felicities, his opposite in elegance, self-assurance and *savoir-faire*. I had been trying to look as though I possessed all those qualities and now I composed my face, giving the impression of the deep and serious consideration his offer merited. The trouble was I didn't want to become anyone's mistress. I might have pleaded the differences in our ages – he was many years older than I – but my wits had deserted me. Finally I came up with the excuse that I was promised to another. When Paddy enquired what my affianced did for a living, I looked wildly round the dining-room for inspiration and hit on the avocation 'waiter'. When Paddy enquired where this paragon waited I muttered, 'The Isle of Man.'

For some reason I could never fathom, the mention of the Isle of Man was like a red rag to a bull. Paddy banged the table with his fist so that the fine bone china danced, while the rest of the room looked askance. 'Jesus Christ,' he swore. 'To think that Ireland's leading poet should be turned down for a waiter working in the Isle of Man!' He spat out the name with such venom that I began to wonder had his mother been molested there or was it a place of such bestial excesses that no decent person would visit, let alone take employment, there. I expected him to sweep the linen and glass from the table, to hurl the wine on the floor and to attack the unfortunate waiter who at that moment was attempting to *flambé* our Crêpes Suzette. Fortunately he contained himself, merely flinging a handful of notes on the table and storming out of the room. I followed meekly. I couldn't think what else to do.

Paddy insisted on seeing me home and, as we made our way past the gates of Trinity College in search of public transport, the enormity of my confession seemed to hit him again. He stopped to attack me verbally, to the delight of a couple of children who had to be dragged away by irate parents who protested that they had never heard such language. To give Paddy his due, he apologised a few days later, adding that it was my own fault for keeping him waiting for over an hour so that he was in a lather of nerves and drink by the time I arrived. I am glad to say we remained good friends down the years. My most abiding memory is of meeting him accidentally at the Curragh shortly before he died, on a cold and miserable day when I shared a packet of sandwiches and a flask of phase, I still most enjoy a glass of sherry before a meal. Paddy was not the guest of honour that night; that distinction fell to Larus Sigurbjorensen, Director of the National Theatre of Reykjavik, Iceland, on a flying visit to Ireland. Even if Paddy wasn't the most important visitor in Delargy's eyes, he was an object of interest to everyone else. We all knew that in his early twenties and with hardly a penny in his pocket, let alone the price of the train fare, he had walked the eighty miles from Monaghan to Dublin to meet George Russell, better known as Æ, who had published three of his early poems in the *Irish Statesman*. At their meeting Æ loaded Paddy with books and gave him the name of Helen Waddell as a possible patron. Later, when in 1933 Æ shook the dust of Dublin from his feet to live in London, Frank O'Connor became Paddy's mentor and friend.

I shall never forget that night in Delargy's study with a roaring fire and outside the snow falling, falling softly, covering town and country, while Paddy in his gruff Monaghan accent told us of his youth in Mucker in the parish of Inniskeen, halfway between Carrickmacross and Dundalk. Growing up in Inniskeen in the early days of the century was like being caught in a medieval timewarp. Television was a long way in the future, the talkies had still to be invented and the only local entertainment when the day's work was done was a game of football or pitch and toss. Storytelling was common and people still believed in fairies, evil spirits and the return of the dead. Paddy said that the whole of Inniskeen had heard the banshee lamenting on the night his grandfather died.

This was William Carleton country, though he was born

about forty miles away in the Clogher Valley of County Tyrone. A mile from Kavanagh's mother's place was Wild Goose Lodge where one of the most gruesome incidents in the tortured history of agrarian protest took place around 1816. A family said to be informers were trapped in their home, which was set alight by a band of Ribbonmen, who like Moonlighters and Peep O'Day Boys conducted campaigns of cattle maiming, burnings and assassinations against those whom they regarded as oppressors. William Carleton describes in 'Wild Goose Lodge', one of his *Traits and Stories of the Irish Peasantry* (1830, 1833), the burning of the lodge in graphic semifictional detail. His own family had been evicted in 1813 and he joined the secret society for a while. Sometime around 1818 he made his way to Dublin, renounced Catholicism for Protestantism and turned to writing, some of it anti-Catholic. His work gives the finest and most vivid picture of Irish rural life before the Famine.

The story of the burning of the lodge became part of southeast Ulster folklore. 'I heard it long before I ever read or heard of William Carleton,' Paddy said, and gave us the oral version, which Sigurbjorensen noted down and afterwards made into a play for Radio Reykjavik. Carleton had written a highly emotive version. Paddy's was low-key and all the more chilling for that. He began by describing the night in midwinter when forty desperate men gathered in the local chapel where they drank poteen and vowed vengeance on all informers. Then, having taken an oath, they set out in a storm of wind and rain to the doomed lodge. Paddy said his forebears quenched the light in their cottage as they saw the company of men go

Education and Finance, so that they could see for themselves that we weren't squandering on high living the slender grant-in-aid they allowed us. Delargy continually objected to my radio work but I needed the money, and in addition I loved the theatre and theatre folk amongst whom I made many friends.

One of my favourite actresses was Ginette Waddell whose family came from Belfast and whose father Sam (1878–1967) was better known as the playwright 'Rutherford Mayne'. Her aunt Helen Waddell was a beautiful woman and a formidable scholar, best known for her passionate novel *Peter Abelard* (1933), which had become a bestseller, praised by, among others, Bernard Shaw. After publication, Helen was lionised by London society, invited to lunch by Ramsay MacDonald's cabinet and to tea in Buckingham Palace in the company of J. M. Barrie, of *Peter Pan* fame, and the governor of the Bank of England.

Peter Abelard, which is based on fact, tells the deeply moving story of the twelfth-century lovers, Héloïse and Abélard. He was the undisputed master of Philosophy and Theology in the Paris schools, the most brilliant thinker of his age. Students came from all over Europe to attend his disquisitions: Bretons, Burgundians, Franks, Sicilians, Romans, Germans, Flemish, English, and even a handful of Malachy's men from Armagh. In the fateful fortieth year of his life Abélard was accommodated in the Notre Dame cloisters by Canon Fulbert as tutor to his brilliant eighteen-year-old niece Héloïse. Thrown together, the two began a passionate affair, were married secretly and a son was born. Fulbert took a terrible revenge. He bribed

Abélard's servant to drug his master and had him cas-
trated by a physician. Later Abélard would be condemned
as a heretic and made to burn his writings and he would
end his days as a Cluniac monk while Héloïse became
abbess of the convent at Argenteuil. When she died, her
body was buried by his side in Brittany and their remains
were later reinterred in the Père Lachaise cemetery in
Paris in 1817.

Ginette introduced me to her aunt on an autumn
afternoon. This was the woman that Paddy Kavanagh had
spoken of in such glowing terms, in her early fifties,
striking-looking with expressive eyes and silver hair. She
wore a moss green frock, amber beads and a silver-fox
fur which she said she had worn to tea with Queen Mary.
I discovered that she was an incurable romantic and had
found herself engaged to four men at the same time. Her
poem 'I Shall Not Go to Heaven', which describes a
possible paradise in a cottage in the Mourne mountains,
was written for one of them:

> *Would you think Heaven could be so small a thing*
> *As a lit window on the hills at night?*
> *And come in stumbling from the gloom,*
> *Half-blind, into a firelit room,*
> *Turn, and see you,*
> *And there abide.*

I told her how much that poem had moved me when I first
read it. Her Mourne mountain man, as she called him, had
been in love with her since girlhood, but on graduating from
Queen's she had spent ten years nursing her stepmother and

then continued with her education at Oxford, as she had promised her clergyman father. 'After that', she said, 'it was too late.' She continued as she stirred her tea, half in a dream: 'It's a queer world; there were the men who loved me all wasted and me who could have loved terribly and was born to have a house and children, living up four flights of stairs writing a book. That first night in London I went to bed defeated and as I lay in the dark I heard a voice speaking the first verse:

> *I shall not go to Heaven when I die,*
> > *But if they'll let me be*
> *I think I'll take the road I used to know*
> > *That goes by Shere-na-garagh and the sea.*

And in the morning I remembered the poem and wrote it down.'

A year after parting with the Mourne man, she walked into the offices of Constable the publishers and met Otto Kyllmann, the Director and Chairman, twenty years her senior, who was to be such an influence in her life. 'He was a brilliant conversationalist, cultured, courteous and expensive in his tastes.' He was Bernard Shaw's publisher, having taken over from Archibald Constable. 'I was thirty-six years of age,' Helen continued, 'old enough to have sense, and besides he was married with an invalid wife, though he lived a bachelor life in rented apartments.' Their friendship deepened into love and when she bought a house in Primrose Hill, near Regent's Park, he went to live with her until his death in 1959. Six years later it was her turn. I often wonder if her spirit took the road that winds by Shere-na-garagh and the sea to her Mourne man. I like to think it did.

Then it was my turn to offer a confidence. She asked me if I had ever been in love, and for the first and only time I told my story. I was eighteen and he was twice my age. He came to the house to give me a grind for an examination I was taking and from the moment he held my hands in his, I knew I was lost. He had been married before we met but it was a disaster from the word go. They lived apart and he promised me that one day everything would work out. It never did. He made wild plans: we would go to America where he had brothers who had done well in politics. But the war dragged on and then it was 1948 and we were both worn out. It was I who made the break, on New Year's Day 1949. He took it badly and said I had used him, wrung him dry. A month later he was killed in an accident when a drunken driver swerved and hit his car head-on. Afterwards, when I had recovered somewhat, I realised my luck. I had never got pregnant, which was a miracle in itself, given the times we lived in, and I could lose myself in work.

Before we parted, Helen asked after Paddy Kavanagh, who had unwisely taken a libel action against *The Leader*, a weekly magazine, in 1953. A notorious law case followed in which a hostile jury found against him, though he was granted a retrial. Before he could fight it, however, disaster struck again; he was diagnosed as having cancer and had to have a lung removed. On polling day in the general election of 1954, John A. Costello, who had been Taoiseach from 1948 to 1951 and a trenchant defence counsel in Paddy's action, met him coming out of a polling-booth. They shook hands and Costello expressed the hope that Paddy did not hold any resentment against him over his gruelling cross-examination. Paddy laughed. 'Resentment? I have just voted for you!' So impressed was Costello that in 1957, with the help of the UCD President Michael Tierney, he secured a post for Paddy in the Extra-Mural Department of UCD. Paddy was to be paid £300 a year for lectures on poetry. This near-sinecure continued until his death in 1967.

Helen had first met Paddy when she opened the door of 32 Primrose Hill one afternoon to find a shabby young man standing on the doorstep with a letter of introduction from Æ. She arranged that he meet the publishers Michael Joseph who encouraged him and later published his autobiography, *The Green Fool* (1938). He was penniless when they met. She told me that evening that she had given him sufficient money to take him back to Dublin, pay his rent and keep him going in cigarettes and food while he wrote his book. While Paddy constantly spoke of Helen's goodness, he never revealed that he had paid back every penny of the money. Helen used the cheque to send a needy nineteen-year-old girl with a sick mother to a Brighton hotel for a much-needed rest. Shortly afterwards the mother died and the girl went to Australia where she made a happy marriage.

'It's odd how things turn out,' Helen said to me that evening as we parted. 'But for Paddy's integrity in returning the money I had given him and which I never expected to see again, I would probably have done nothing to help that girl.' Then she turned on me her brilliant smile and asked, 'Was it fate?'

22

THE END OF THE QUEST

The sixties were the years of change. I gave up radio work
and in my spare time wrote a page in the *Sunday Press*.
At first Delargy objected strenuously to my journalism,
as was his wont, until District-Justice Liam Price, an
influential member of the board of the Commission and
his close friend, said that he looked forward to my weekly
articles, that they were light and amusing and helped him
digest his morning bacon and eggs. After that, nothing
more was said. I had some excuse for my incursion into
journalism: times were never so good, yet we in the
Commission were still being paid a pittance. It was no
fault of Delargy. The grant-in-aid was so small that it
allowed for no increments, no promotion, no severance
pay, compulsory retirement on marriage for women (at
that stage still a feature of Irish employment) and, hardest
of all, no pension rights. One of the full-time folklore
collectors, Seán Ó Cróinín, had died suddenly in 1959,
leaving behind him a wife and family. His dependants
were given the two weeks' salary due and that was all.
Within a year the widow was dead. It made the remainder

of the staff, particularly the men with families, very unsettled. I too began to think that it was time for a change or that maybe I might get married.

Nils, a Swedish professor and distinguished linguist, first came to Ireland some time after the war to study the various types of Irish spoken in County Clare. He was a tall man with Nordic good looks. He had travelled the world and could as easily converse with the North American Indians or tribes living in the Amazon basin as he did with Africans, Eskimos, Irish speakers of different dialects or other minority groups whose languages were dying out. It was said that he could master any language in six weeks, but of all the different people he had met, he had the closest affinity with the Irish – or so he believed. I have found this to be true of many Scandinavians and sometimes wonder if it is the result of race memory. When the Vikings of the tenth and eleventh centuries raided Ireland (which they did time and time again) they brought back to the north not only monastic treasures and the proceeds of the sackings of town and country but also Irish captives, men and women, whom they either kept or sold as slaves. And when they founded Dublin and other Irish cities, they continued to intermarry with the natives until they were defeated. Then some took ship to Bristol, the Isle of Man and the Orkneys, where they had strongholds, or returned north with their Irish wives and children.

I had not yet disentangled myself from my first love affair when I met Nils. For some reason I accepted his invitation to the comedy film *Whisky Galore* at the De Luxe Cinema in Camden Street. The story was based on an incident that had happened during the war when a ship, the SS *Cabinet Minister*, ran aground in the Hebrides. Its cargo of whisky was acquired by the Todday islanders in spite of the efforts of HM Customs and Excise and they were very happy until supplies ran out. Nils was of a serious frame of mind but he enjoyed the film enormously. Afterwards we had supper in the Unicorn Restaurant in Merrion Row which continued to be UCD's informal staff club for as long as the college remained in Earlsfort Terrace.

Nils told me that night that he was completely happy. Out of the blue he proposed marriage to me on the way home. I was startled and flattered but refused his offer. I liked him well but, as I have said, my heart was not mine to give; besides, he had a foreignness about him, like the speck in the yoke of an egg, that somehow put me off. After that first encounter, he came to Ireland each summer, regular as the returning swallow. I continued to sidestep his overtures, though we remained good friends. He once said that for him I epitomised Ireland. In the family it was always believed that I took after my father's mother. She was Catherine Tierney from Galway and was known to the family as the 'Irish rose'. I had none of her great good looks, except her dark curly hair and hazel eyes, but I spoke Irish and had made a name of sorts for myself writing Irish fairytales. These are the kind of things that can bewitch a foreign visitor.

I only mention this love affair because of a strange incident after it came to an end. I had finally given Nils and myself the chance to find out if the friendship between us could develop into something deeper. My colleague and best friend, Catriona Ó Ruadháin, had recently got engaged to a well known sportswriter on one of the national dailies. I was to be bridesmaid and was soon caught up in all the wedding excitement. With Catriona urging me on, I accepted Nils's tentative invitation to dinner the June evening he arrived in Dublin. He was so startled when I agreed to go out with him that he dropped his suitcase on my foot.

After that the romance at last took off. We went walking the Wicklow hills, saw the moon rising over Howth Head, fed the animals in the Zoological Gardens, bathed in Killiney and had dinner most nights in the Unicorn. It was a marvellous summer and I found to my surprise that Nils was a tender and passionate lover. I agreed to marry him but had no wish to live in Sweden and hoped that he could get himself fixed up in Dublin. He tried for a post in the Institute of Advanced Studies but that year they were short of funds. Much as they would have welcomed his scholarship, they had to refuse. Maybe next year things would be better, they said.

I parted with Nils at the beginning of autumn. He was on his way to the Hebrides and I wrote a few days later to his Scottish address saying I was sorry but I was too old to tear up my roots in Ireland, too old to make a life with him that would entail travelling to out-of-the-way places and meeting people whose language I could never hope to understand. Or maybe it was that I wasn't in love with him after all or that my first love affair had spoiled me for anyone else. I just do not know.

Our letters crossed in the post. His was strange, distraught, quite untypical of the sober, scholarly man I knew so well. He wrote of skeletons and how he had a foreboding that a letter from me was on the way, bringing bad news. He had had a dream the night before: he found himself in a long lean boat, headed fore and aft, a Danish keel on a Viking raiding party to Ireland. Twenty-four oars, twelve rowers, a cluster of vermilion shields draped along the boat's low flanks, and the rest of the Norse ships not far behind. 'I knew what the outcome would be,' he continued. 'We would sack every town and village, and you would be killed with many more of your kith and kin. I also knew I would search for you again and again down the centuries. Maybe we shall meet in another life.'

I shivered when I read that letter. Nils, like many Scandinavians, was pagan at heart. I had no idea that he believed in a life beyond the one we know but he did tell me that most primitive people and indeed many religious believed in reincarnation or the transmigration of souls. We had discussed how this belief was true of the pagan Irish and how the early sagas bore this out.

The wooing of Etain, as we have seen, tells how one of the immortals is changed into a golden fly and is then reborn as a human child. In a later tale Liban the Mermaid of Lough Neagh lives out different lives, as a young girl and a mermaid in the lake, finally to regain her human shape as an old woman. Before she dies she is baptised by St Patrick so that she is sure of immortality in heaven. Common too in old Irish literature is the theme of the hero who is reborn many times, as a warrior, a salmon, a hind, a stag, and a great boar roaming the forest until his final reincarnation as a prince.

As for Nils – after that summer he did not come back

to Ireland and I never saw him again. Soon after his return to Sweden, he married one of his students. I hope they were happy.

Before the sixties were out, most of the great story-tellers were gone the 'way of truth'. Dwindled away too was the number of correspondents and part-time workers who helped us collect what remained of the folklore of the country. True, short questionnaires on specialised subjects continued to be sent out but the excitements of the early days were over, the race against time almost run. Television had come to Ireland and the world was a different place.

I remember a cartoon in the *Dublin Opinion* (1922–68), the humorous magazine that had kept the country laughing for years. It showed an old man seated beside the fire muttering to himself the familiar opening of a folktale, '*Fadó, fadó*', while the remainder of his family sat with their backs turned, their eyes glued to the television set and paying him no heed. Like much humour it had its barb, even heartbreak. It was sad to think that great folktales of the past, some of which had crossed oceans and deserts and were older than the Pyramids, had been buried with the storytellers, men and women who had at the end of their days inevitably become figures of fun. I remembered what extraordinary memories such people had, how they first heard the tales as children, listening to their elders while hiding under the kitchen table or crouched on the stairs leading to the attic where they shared their sleeping-quarters with fishing tackle and farming instruments – sometimes even domestic fowl. They would assimilate those folktales word for word, some longer than the modern 'blockbuster', often taking seven nights in the telling.

I vividly recalled the 'runs' that occurred here and there in the story and gave the teller time to gather his thoughts for the next adventure that the hero and his companions would meet:

> *Away and away they rode, by hills and hollows and thorny ways, by shimmering loughs and shining streams, farther away than I could tell you and twice the distance that you could tell me.*

Often the storyteller finished his tale with a popular passage, at which point the listeners, having heard it many times before, joined in:

> *They returned home and held a feast that lasted seven days and seven nights. I was there with them but if I was the devil a taste of the feast did they give me. All I got from them was paper shoes and stockings of thick milk. I threw them back at them. They were drowned and I came safe. Not a word or news have I got from them for the past year and a day.*

At this, the man of the house would stand up to show that the night's storytelling was at the end and, crossing himself, make the prayer

> *May the company and myself be seven thousand times better off a year from today. And the dear*

blessings of God and of the Church on the souls of the dead. Amen.

The sixties were also the decade in which I went to America and was tempted to stay. I had been invited by my friend and mentor, Arthur Hutson, Dean of the English Faculty at Berkeley, University of California, and his wife Elizabeth, to be their guest. Their house on San Luis Road had the best possible view in Berkeley. From the window of the living-room it was possible to see San Francisco away in the distance with Mount Diabolo across the bay forming a backdrop, at a distance of sixteen miles or more. UCD at Belfield had not yet been built and Berkeley was the biggest campus I had ever seen. I was intrigued by the casual behaviour of the students (taken for granted in Ireland today), who thought nothing of putting their feet on the backs of chairs or walking out of a lecture if they got bored.

When they heard I was from Ireland, they demanded that I tell them ghost stories. Some were second or third generation Irish who had heard from their people of the 'hungry grass', so called because it is generally believed that during the Great Famine some unfortunate soul expired of hunger on that spot. I said that there were hundreds of accounts of this in the archives of the Commission and that two of my friends had had the experience of 'going astray'. One was Séamus Ennis, who at the time was collecting folk music in Macroom in west Cork. Coming home from a wake one night he was suddenly overcome with the most terrible hunger and collapsed on the ground. He was found in the early morning by a passing farmer, who revived him with milk and left him home. I told them of Anna of the Bluestacks who had given me the griddle cake lest a similar fate should overcome me.

David Thomson tells of an experience he had when he was at Woodbrook. One night he drove a pet lamb into a paddock, a place he knew blindfold. After shutting the gate, he could not find the hole in the fence to get out. He appeared to lose his way, walked round in circles for hours on end, as though wandering in endless space, but never reaching fence or wall. At last he lay down on the grass, which was damp and cold, and slept for a bit. When he awoke it was morning and he walked straight back to the house without doubting the direction. I told the students that 'going astray' was common in Ireland. Certain fields were known to have a 'stray', a lost soul or the grave of an unbaptised baby. Some believed that the fairies would put you astray but the most prevalent belief was that it had to do with the Famine.

Another story the students clamoured to hear was that of the 'headless' coach. Many said that their parents or other near relatives had witnessed this spectacle, and they wanted to know its origin. The headless coach was usually associated with notorious landlords or magistrates who abused their powers, and was customarily seen near their homes. Because of the resemblance between these ghostly carriages and actual horsedrawn hearses, they were interpreted as a sign of death. They had come from the 'other world' to bring back people from this life. If the nocturnal coach touched a person or spattered blood on him, it was an indication that he would die soon after.

To safeguard themselves, people lay face down on the ground or turned their coats inside out so that they would not be recognised.

During my stay in Berkeley I was overwhelmed by hospitality. The goodwill and generosity of these Americans put us to shame and I sighed for a return of the days when Irish hospitality was accepted as a way of life. Even the Vikings, marauders and hatchetmen as they were, expressed astonishment at the surpassing hospitality of the Irish. In the Icelandic sagas it is recorded how the Irish built their houses at crossroads to encourage travellers to come and eat with them. What is stranger still is that these men from the north were so intrigued with this custom, they introduced it into their homeland.

Each time I was invited to an American home, corned beef and cabbage (still regarded as a festive Irish meal) appeared somewhere on the menu. Irish whiskey, too, was popular and one of my hosts went so far as to produce a bottle of poteen, which he had been given in Ireland the year before, and in the age-old manner spilled three preliminary drops to placate the Good People. I was offered a job at the university but I felt I could all too easily spend the remainder of my life telling ghost stories or fairytales to the students; that and the prospect of corned beef and cabbage each time I was invited to dine was too much. I decided it was time I went home.

At the airport in San Francisco I met Robert Kennedy on his way to a meeting in Los Angeles. I was en route home via New York. He told me his brother, the late president, had never been happier than on his last visit to Ireland, that when he was depressed he would watch a film his aides had made during his time here. Robert was interested to hear that I was a folklorist. His parting words were that he was looking forward to coming to Ireland the following summer and that he would call into the Commission's offices and see what material we had from his ancestral home county, Wexford. I promised I would have the manuscripts ready and waiting. Halfway across the Atlantic the captain came out of the cockpit to announce that Robert had been shot in Los Angeles. It was 5 June 1968 and he died the next day. I wrote about my encounter with him when I got back to Dublin, and the story was carried on radio and television.

As I have said, the 'swinging' sixties were a time of change. For us at the Irish Folklore Commission it was also the end of an era. Michael Tierney had with great foresight pushed for the creation of a new campus for UCD at Belfield. A member of our board and a lifelong friend of Delargy, he arranged for us to be housed in the new Arts block as the Department of Irish Folklore. Our main work would be cataloguing and editing the material we had gathered for publication, as well as preparing students for a degree in Irish Folklore, but the archives and the library would always be open to the people of Ireland, who had contributed so much. We would be rewarded with decent salaries and given credit for pension purposes for our years of work.

I was to spend seventeen years researching and lecturing in Belfield. I enjoyed the students and staff but it was never the same as in the early years when we were young, enthusiastic and imbued with Séamus Delargy's dedication and sense of urgency, and the belief that the work would live after us and was well worth the doing. Delargy spoke for us all when, at the official opening of the Department of Irish Folklore at Belfield on 28 September 1971, he quoted a favourite passage from the Canadian Farley Mowat's *The People of the Deer* (1954):

My journey was over but I was still tied to the Barren not by the simple web of memory alone, but by something more powerful. There was, and is, an abiding affection in my heart for the men and women who lent me their eyes so that I was privileged to look backward through the dark void of years, and to see not only the relics of forgotten times, but also into the minds and thoughts of the men of those times. It was a great gift I had from the people and one that deserved a repayment.

SELECT BIBLIOGRAPHY

Carbery, Mary. *The Farm by Lough Gur*. London, 1938.

Carleton, William. *Traits and Stories of the Irish Peasantry*. Dublin, 1830, 1833.

Coakley, Denis. *Oscar Wilde, The Importance of Being Irish*. Dublin, 1994.

Corrigan, Felicitas. *Helen Waddell*. London, 1986.

Cross, Eric. *The Tailor and Ansty*. Dublin, 1942.

Cross and Slover. *Ancient Irish Tales*. New York, 1910.

Danaher, Kevin. *The Year in Ireland*. Cork, 1972.

Eliot, Marc. *Walt Disney, Hollywood's Dark Prince*. London, 1994.

Flower, Robin. *The Western Island*. Oxford, 1944.

Hyde, Douglas. *Beside the Fire*. London, 1890.

Laverty, Maura. *Never No More*. London, 1942.

Lysaght, Patricia. *The Banshee*. Dublin, 1986.

Mac Liammóir, Micheál. *All for Hecuba*. London, 1946.

MacNeill, Máire. *The Festival of Lughnasa*. Dublin, 1986.

Mahon, Bríd. *Land of Milk and Honey*. Dublin, 1991.

—————. *Traditional Dyestuffs in Ireland*. Dublin, 1983.

—————. *The Wonder Tales of Ireland*. Dublin, 1975.

O'Connor, Frank. *The Stories of Frank O'Connor*. London, 1951.

Ó Duilearga, Séamus. *Leabhar Sheain Í Chonaill*. Dublin, 1948.

—————————. *The Gaelic Storyteller*. London, 1945.

Ó Súilleabháin, Seán. *A Handbook of Irish Folklore*. Dublin, 1942.

—————————. *Irish Wake Amusements*. Cork, 1967.

Sayers, Peg. *Machtnamh Seana-Mhná (An Old Woman's Reflections)*. London, 1962.

Thomson, David. *Woodbrook*. London, 1974.

Tolkien, J. R. R. *The Hobbit*. London, 1937.

Woodham-Smith, Cecil. *The Great Hunger*. London, 1962.

INDEX